Robert Burns

1759–96

A Portrait of Scotland's National Bard with a selection of his songs and verse

by Elisabeth Fraser

To Dr John Moore, Burns wrote
from Mauchline on 2 August 1787:

'It is ever my opinion that the great, unhappy mistakes and blunders both in a rational and religious point of view, of which we see thousands daily guilty are owing to their ignorance or mistaken notions of themselves. To know myself had been all along my constant study. I weighed myself alone; I balanced myself with others; I watched every means of information, how much ground I occupied both as a man and as a poet; I studied assiduously Nature's design – where she seemed to have intended the various lights and shades in my character.'

JARROLD
PUBLISHING

Acknowledgements

I would like to thank all those who have generously given their help and advice during the preparation of this book: James A Mackay, former editor of the *Burns Chronicle*, for allowing his Subscribers' Edition of *The Complete Works of Robert Burns* (1986) to be used as a source for the poems and songs; Shirley Bell, Chief Executive of The Robert Burns World Federation Ltd, for providing the text and coat of arms on pp. 28–9; John Inglis, Honorary Archivist of The Robert Burns World Federation Ltd for checking the text and providing valuable information and advice; the Irvine Burns Club for allowing access to their archives and reproduction of images in their possession (pp. 11, 13, 25 (bottom), 33, 49, 50 and outside back cover); Doreen Kean, Reference Services Manager of Glasgow City Council's Cultural and Leisure Services for providing the photograph of and information on the Mitchell Library's manuscript of 'Auld Lang Syne' (p. 97); The National Trust for Scotland for permission to reproduce photographs taken on their property; Dame Jean Scott for helping to provide the photograph on p. 14; Tom McIlwraith, Past President of The Burns Federation, for permitting reproduction of the print on p. 20 (below); and John Manson, Curator of the Burns Cottage Museum, Alloway.

Picture credits

The publisher is grateful to the following for their kind permission to reproduce images: Abbotsford Collection, Melrose: p. 14; Alloway Publishing: p. 12 (top); Burns National Heritage Park, Alloway: pp. 64, 71/outside front cover (top left), 88; The City of Edinburgh Council, on loan to the Scottish National Portrait Gallery: p. 19 (bottom); Dumfries and Galloway Tourist Board/'Great Scot': p. 25 (top); Dumfries Museum: pp. 22 (right), 24; Mary Evans Picture Library: p. 85; National Galleries of Scotland: pp. 1/outside front cover (centre), 4, 9 (top), 18, 21, 34, 46, 74; The National Trust for Scotland: pp. 6, 8 (both) and 77; Tony Stone Images/Marcus Brooke: p. 89.

Photographs taken for Jarrold Publishing: Mike Bisset: outside front cover (bottom), pp. 5, 8, 9 (bottom), 10, 11, 13, 25 (bottom), 40, 42, 49, 50, 61, 62, 73, 86; John Curtis: p. 22 (left); Max Mackenzie: p. 20.

Outside front cover: Painting by W H Midwood of Robert Burns presenting a bible to Mary Campbell (top left); Brig o' Doon, Alloway (top right); Burns Cottage, Alloway (bottom); detail from a portrait of Robert Burns by Alexander Nasmyth (1758–1840), painted in 1787 (centre)

Inside front cover: An 18th-century engraving of Edinburgh Castle from the Vennel

Title page: Robert Burns by Alexander Nasmyth (detail, as cover)

Outside back cover: Burns and the Vision. This painting by James Elder Christie (1847–1914) depicts Burns seated at his fireside in Mossgiel and being visited by his Muse, whom he refers to as 'Coila' (a corruption of 'Kyle', the Ayrshire district where he was born) –

'And wear thou this' – She solemn said,
And bound the holly round my head:
The polish'd leaves and berries red
    Did rustling play;
And, like a passing thought, she fled
    In light away.
           (Last verse of 'The Vision')

ISBN 0-7117-1094-5
© Jarrold Publishing 1999
Designed and produced by Jarrold Publishing, Norwich.
Printed in China. 1/99

Contents

Songs and verses:

3

Introduction

Information about the great Scottish poet Robert Burns has been gathered over the years since his death in 1796; all of it has contributed to portray the life and work of this remarkable man. Above all his letters, in themselves, have assisted scholars not only to understand his poetical works but they have also formed an important insight into his life and character. The Burns family have submitted letters, documents and possessions relating to the poet. Volumes have been written about him. There are records with regard to his military service with the Royal Dumfries Volunteers, his Masonic Lodge connections and his occupation as an excise officer in and around Dumfries. Great works of art have portrayed him in various aspects of his life. The Robert Burns World Federation and the Burns Chronicle play an important part in keeping his memory alive and linking together the many Burns clubs now formed all over the world.

The following synopsis on Burns' life, together with the Burns Country map will help the reader to follow his activities. The songs and poems selected in this book are among Burns' most popular. We hope that the reader will be inspired to make a closer contact with the many places related to this unique Scottish Bard, and to gain a deeper insight into his works.

Left: Burns Cottage, Alloway, the poet's birthplace
Opposite: *Robert Burns* by Alexander Nasmyth, painted in 1828

Scotland's National Bard

ROBERT BURNS, one of the greatest, some feel the greatest, of Scottish poets of the 18th century had and still has a profound influence on the literary world. He was undoubtedly a genius, with a remarkable talent for portraying the truth of what he saw in daily life. His 'innocent' mind enabled him to capture in words the exact truth, without any thought of the consequence.

The poet was born on 25 January 1759 in Alloway, near Ayr. When his father was riding to fetch a doctor to assist at Robert's birth, it is said he helped an old gypsy woman to cross a flooded stream. In gratitude, she visited the new-born baby, gave him her blessing and predicted his fame.

Statues of characters from 'Tam o Shanter' in Souter Johnnie's Cottage, Kirkoswald

The cottage of his birth, which was built by his father, is now world famous. Originally it was under the care of the Trustees of Burns Cottage and Monument. Now all Burns properties come under the title of Burns National Heritage Park, although the Trustees still play an important role. In 1898 the Trustees built a separate museum close by the cottage to house priceless paintings, manuscripts and other documents and objects associated with the poet and his family. Over the years more rooms have been added to house the increased collections, as well as many other visitor attractions.

To celebrate the birth of this great poet, Burns Suppers are held – a unique commemoration afforded to no other poet. These famous suppers originated in Burns Cottage, when nine of Burns' friends met and had supper there in 1801. Today, they are held all over the world, nowhere more so than in Scotland. His world-acclaimed song 'Auld Lang Syne', always sung at these suppers, has the penetrating quality of bringing people together wherever they may be.

Within walking distance of the Cottage at Alloway is the Tam o' Shanter Experience, based on the poem. This three-screen audio-visual production reveals the exceptional talent of the Scottish Bard. It is claimed he wrote this poem at Ellisland in a single day. A little further down the road from the Tam o' Shanter Experience is the Burns Monument, set in a beautiful garden close to the Brig o' Doon and the Auld Kirk.

Contemporary fame

It is hard to imagine today what the 18th century held for such a genius. There was little or no mass media or public relations to aid such a talent. Burns had to rely on friends and acquaintances for their introductions to learned men. With little money and only a farming background, this was by no means easy. Yet, Burns did gain a favourable reputation during his lifetime both for his verse and his songs, and he was received by the highest society of the day.

To labour bred

When Burns was six years old, his father, William Burnes, engaged a young teacher, John Murdoch, to set up a small school in Alloway. The school was organised to take some local children in addition to the Burnes family (they later changed their surname to Burns). John Murdoch, who became the lifelong friend of the poet, received from Burns the highest tribute a schoolmaster could wish from his pupil. 'I have not forgotten, nor will I ever forget, the many obligations I lie under to your kindness and friendship.' When Burns was not in the schoolroom, he was helping his father on their farm and at the age of 14 years became the principal labourer, for William Burnes employed no hired hands. The poet wrote of this period: 'The cheerless gloom of a hermit, with the unceasing moil of a galley-slave, brought me to my sixteenth year, a little before which I committed the sin of rhyme.'

Surveying mankind

In his 17th year (1775) Burns spent the summer at Kirkoswald learning higher mathematics and surveying at Hugh Rodger's School. But during this period of his life Burns felt he had made more progress in the understanding of mankind than he ever had from his lessons. Today, at Kirkoswald in the restored alehouse in the garden of Souter [cobbler] Johnnie's Cottage, now under the care of the National Trust for Scotland, there are life-size stone

Above and below: Interior and exterior of the Bachelors' Club, Tarbolton

Above: The Inauguration of Burns as Poet Laureate of the Lodge Canongate, Kilwinning, 1787 *by William Stewart Watson*

sculptures of the characters portrayed in Burns' famous poem 'Tam o Shanter'.

Bachelors' Club and Freemasons

In 1780 a few of the young men of Tarbolton formed themselves into a literary and debating society with Burns as their president. The building where they held their meetings was called the Bachelors' Club and is now under the care of the National Trust for Scotland.

In the following year the poet was admitted as an apprentice to the Free-masons at St James Lodge in Tarbolton, becoming Deputy-Master of the Lodge on 27 July 1784.

Deception and fire at Irvine

In June 1781 Burns entered into a partnership with his uncle, Alexander Peacock, a flax-dresser in Irvine. This enterprise proved disastrous. The poet said: 'My partner was a scoundrel of the first water who made money by the mystery of thieving.' The shop was burnt down during the New Year Carousal in 1781. Today, the Heckling Shop, as it was called, has been restored to a state as near the original as possible – including the thatched roof – by North Ayrshire District Council and other interested parties. The shop is within the Glasgow Vennel and is linked with a Studio Gallery Museum and the Ayrshire Writers and Artists Society. The Glasgow Vennel is a cobbled street rich in history, now looking as it was in Burns' day.

Not far from here is 'Wellwood', the Irvine Burns Club, with a fine museum and library – the oldest continuous Burns club in the world. One of the rare first editions of Burns' poems, printed in Kilmarnock, together with

Above: The Heckling Shop, Glasgow Vennel, Irvine

9

Above: Glasgow Vennel, Irvine

six of the original manuscripts, form part of the invaluable collection.

Death of Burns' father

Burns returned to Tarbolton to help with Lochlea farm. Unfortunately, his father developed a lingering illness and died on 13 February 1784. Much affected by this, Burns wrote of his father: 'the tender father, and generous friend now at rest from the many buffetings of an evil world, against which he so long and so bravely struggled'. (See 'My Father was a Farmer' on p. 46.)

Farming and romance at Mauchline

In 1784 Gilbert, his brother, and Robert subleased the farm of Mossgiel, near Mauchline. The farm was of some

118 acres (48 ha), and every member of the family who laboured on the farm received a wage. It was at Mauchline that Burns came into contact with men of a position somewhat better than his own. He was now 25 years old, with a great love of life; his clever wit and natural muse made him welcome wherever he went.

It was during 1785 that Burns first met Jean Armour. The romance began through a chance remark made by the poet about his beloved dog. He was heard to say that if he could find a lass as faithful as his dog he would marry her. One day, Jean Armour was laying out some washing on the village bleach green as Burns was passing by; she coyly called to the poet, enquiring if he had found the lass of his dreams. Burns fell deeply in love with Jean. This romantic love affair was destined to bring great anguish and concern to Burns. For when Jean's father heard that his daughter was expecting a baby, he forbade the marriage, refusing to accept Burns' written acknowledgement which, according to Scottish Law, would have been accepted as evidence of an irregular marriage. Jean was sent to Paisley to friends of the family, and this so affected the poet that he made plans to emigrate. He had been offered a job in Jamaica at £30 a year. At the behest of friends Burns decided to publish his

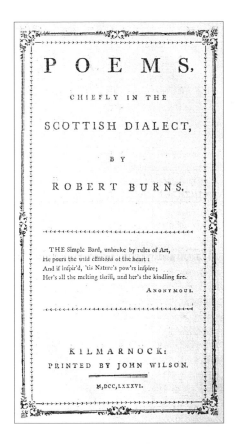

poems by subscription to raise the necessary fare of 9 guineas.

First edition at Kilmarnock

Burns' first edition was published by John Wilson of Kilmarnock, on 31 July 1786, price 3 shillings, and 612 copies were printed. It was an immediate success and a larger edition was called for. Unfortunately, the poet could not raise the £27 to cover the cost of the paper – his first edition had brought him a profit of only £20.

Prior to the Kilmarnock edition being printed, the family agreed to change the spelling of their surname from Burnes to that used in Ayrshire, Burns.

He had already booked his passage to Jamaica when he wrote: 'I had taken farewell of my friends and my chest was on the road to Greenock when I had composed a song "The gloomy night is gathering fast" [p. 42] which was to be my last effort of my muse in Caledonia, when a letter from Dr Blacklock, the blind Edinburgh Poet, to a friend of mine, overthrew all my schemes by arousing my poetic ambitions.'

Mary Campbell

It must have been about this time that Burns formed an attachment with Mary Campbell, though it was not until many years later that her surname was known. The bible, in two small volumes, given to her by Burns is preserved in the monument to Burns at Alloway by the Banks o' Doon; and the painting by W H Midwood (p. 71) shows Burns presenting it to Mary. The original of this painting hangs in Burns Cottage, Alloway.

Into Edinburgh society

Encouraged by Dr Blacklock's praise and his many introductions, Burns set out on horseback for Edinburgh. James Dalrymple of Orangefield, near Monkton, gave the poet an introduction to the Earl of Glencairn. This brought Burns into the centre of the high society of Edinburgh.

Burns never forgot the Earl of Glencairn – his generous patron – and immortalised his name in a beautiful poem mourning his death in 1791:

The Bridegroom may forget the Bride
Was made his wedded wife yestreen,
The monarch may forget the crown
That on his head an hour has been.
The mother may forget the child
That smiles so sweetly on her knee;
But I'll remember thee, Glencairn
And all that thou hast done for me;
For all I have and all I am I owe to thee.

These lines appear below the memorial tablet in Falmouth Parish Church to the memory of James Cunningham, 14th Earl of Glencairn. Burns followed the

Above: James Cunningham, 14th Earl of Glencairn (1749–91)

poem with a touching little prayer in French: 'Oublie moi, Grand Dieu, si Jamais je l'oublie.' (Forget me, O God, if ever I forget him.) A snuff mull presented by the Earl of Glencairn to Robert Burns is on display in Burns House, Dumfries, a prized possession of the Dumfries Burns Club.

Nature and high society

One of the chief pleasures Burns derived from his visits to Edinburgh was his early-morning walks taken in many parts of the outskirts of the city.

Left: Edinburgh from Arthur's Seat, where Burns and Nasmyth loved to walk

In the early spring he often climbed to the top of Arthur's Seat, surveying the silent sun rising in the clear fresh air. His chosen companion on these morning walks was his artist friend Alexander Nasmyth, also an ardent lover of nature.

Burns is known to have stayed in various parts of Edinburgh: plaques over doorways and arches of inns and taverns bear his name today. He was invited to attend many poetical gatherings in the noble households of his day: in particular, by the Duchess of Gordon, who was the leader of fashionable society in Edinburgh; she was heard to say of Burns: 'That no man's conversation ever carried her so completely off her feet'. Mrs Alison Cockburn, another high society lady, wrote to a friend: 'The Town is at

Below: C M Hardie's painting of Burns in Edinburgh, *showing the poet with the Duchess of Gordon*

present agog with the Ploughman Poet, who receives adulation with native dignity, and is the very figure of his profession – strong, but coarse, yet he has a most enthusiastic heart of love.'

Sir Walter Scott encounters Burns

By far the most interesting reminiscences on Burns were made by Sir Walter Scott – then a boy of about 15 years old, who met Burns at the home of the distinguished poet Professor Adam Ferguson.

'We youngsters sat silent, looked and listened,' says Scott; Burns was deeply affected by a picture of a soldier lying

The meeting of Sir Walter Scott, aged 15, and Burns at Sciennes House, Edinburgh. Painting by C M Hardie

dead in the snow, his wife and child on one side and his dog on the other. Beneath the picture some verses were written. Burns enquired who the poet was. 'It chanced,' says Scott, 'that nobody but myself remembered that they occur in a half-forgotten poem by Langhorne, called by the unpromising title of "Justice of Peace". I whispered my information to a friend present, who mentioned it to Burns, who rewarded me with a look and a word, which though of mere civility, I then received, and still recollect with very much pleasure. His person was strong and robust; his manners rustic, not clownish, a sort of dignified plainness and simplicity, which received part of its effects perhaps, from one's knowledge of his extraordinary talent. His features are presented in Mr Nasmyth's picture, but to me it conveys the idea that they are diminished, as if in perspective. I think his countenance was more massive than it looks in any of the portraits. I would have taken the Poet, had I not known what he was, for a very sagacious country farmer of the Old Scottish School; i.e. none of your modern agriculturists, who keep labourers for their drudgery, but the douce gudeman who held his own plough. There was a strong expression of sense and shrewdness in all his lineaments: his eye alone, I think, indicated the poetical character and temperament. It was large and of a dark cast which glowed, I say literally glowed, when he spoke with feeling or interest. I never saw such another eye in a human head, though I have seen the most distinguished men of my time. His conversation expressed perfect confidence, without the slightest presumption. Among the men who were the most learned of their time and country, he expressed himself with perfect firmness, but without the least intrusive forwardness. When he differed in opinion, he did not hesitate to express it firmly, yet at the same time with modesty.' Scott continues: 'He was like a farmer dressed in his best to dine with the Laird. I do not speak *in malam partem*, when I say, I never saw a man when in the company with his superiors in station and information more perfectly free from either the reality or the affectation of embarrassment.'

Clarinda

Burns gained many friends during his lifetime, but none dearer to him than Clarinda, Mrs Agnes (Nancy) Maclehose, whom he met in Edinburgh. He admired her capabilities very much. Not only was she a poet but also a promising artist, so they had much in common. Her fascinating charm completely captured the poet's imagination. She was a lady of rank and position, who recognised the poet's incredible talent and encouraged him accordingly. There is little doubt that one of the greatest love-songs ever written was addressed to Clarinda in 'Ae Fond Kiss' (see p. 35).

Second edition

Prior to Burns' meeting with Clarinda, the second edition of his poems was published by William Creech of Edinburgh in April 1787. Much later, when Burns finally settled with Creech, he sold his copyright for 100 guineas.

He received a further £400, £180 of which he gave to his brother Gilbert for support of the family at Mossgiel.

In spite of the excitement of town life, Burns never forgot Jean Armour; the whole episode had deeply affected him. It is known that Burns saw Jean many times during this period, and he often sought to resolve her father's objections to him.

Borders tour

During one of Burns' visits to Edinburgh, while he was waiting for William Creech to settle the account for his second edition, Burns agreed to make a tour of the Borders with his friend Robert Ainslie. They set off from Edinburgh on horseback on 5 May 1787 in high spirits. The first night of their border tour was spent with Robert Ainslie's family in Duns. On the

Border scenery near Innerleithen

following morning of Sunday, Burns was invited to attend the morning service at Duns parish church with the Ainslie family. When the minister announced his text, Burns noticed Rachel, Robert Ainslie's sister, thumbing through her bible looking for the text. Burns tore a blank page from his bible and wrote the following lines, which he passed to Rachel:

> *Fair maid you need not take the hint*
> *Nor idle texts pursue*
> *'Twas guilty sinners that he meant*
> *Not angels such as you.*

Much refreshed from their pleasant stay, Burns and Ainslie travelled on to Coldstream, Kelso, Jedburgh, Melrose and Selkirk, where they were entertained by numerous members of the local nobility. Continuing their tour, Burns and Ainslie made new acquaintances and renewed their friendships with many people in the surrounding country, which took them to Innerleithen and Galashiels, and eventually to Berwick, Eyemouth and Dunbar, finally ending in Newcastle via Alnwick and Morpeth. Here Burns parted from Ainslie on Sunday, 20 May to make his own way back to Edinburgh by way of Carlisle, Dumfries and Mauchline, where he visited his family.

The poet made several more tours, including one to Stirlingshire and two to the Highlands of Scotland.

Highland tour

Burns' most important and extensive Highland tour was taken with his close friend William Nicol, an Edinburgh schoolteacher. The rugged mountains with their majestic scenery and wildness inspired the poet, then 28 years old, to a greater height of song-writing: nor did he lose this new-found inspiration when he returned to Dumfriesshire, where he settled for the remaining years of his life.

In August 1787 Burns and Nicol set off on their Highland tour for Inverness via Stirling and Dunkeld, returning by way of Aberdeen. In his letter to his brother Gilbert on 17 September 1787, Burns reveals that he passed through Crieff on his way to Kenmore and Aberfeldy. Burns stayed two nights as guest of the 4th Duke of Atholl, and on the 31 August 1787 he dined with the Duchess and her family, noticing the ease of manner of their hosts. Burns was able to walk about the estate and admire, and in some cases criticise, the formal grounds which he found for the most part delightful although sometimes spoilt by bad taste.

After walking around the area of the Bruar Falls, Burns in due course composed the poem 'The Humble Petition of Bruar Water to the Noble Duke of Athole', supposedly a plea from the Bruar to the Duke, of which the following is the fifth verse:

The Bruar Falls 'wi' tow'ring trees'

> *Would then my noblest master please*
> *To grant my highest wishes,*
> *He'll shade my banks wi' tow'ring trees,*
> *And bonie spreading bushes.*
> *Delighted doubly then, my Lord,*
> *You'll wander on my banks,*
> *And listen mony a grateful bird*
> *Return you tuneful thanks.*

This poem was sent by Burns to Joseph Walker, tutor to the Marquis of Tullibardine, son of the Duke of Atholl, while Burns was in Inverness on 5 September 1787. His Grace lost no time in responding to the plea to clothe

Niel Gow – the Dunkeld Fiddler, painted by Sir Henry Raeburn in 1787

the banks in trees, and the policy has continued to the present day.

It was at Dunkeld that Burns visited the famous fiddler Niel Gow in his home. It is certain that he had a great influence on Burns' song-writing, for it is known that he played many a reel for the poet. Incidentally, Burns also played the fiddle, which must have been a considerable advantage when writing his songs. He continued his journey 'in those enchanting days', visiting Sir James Grant of Grant Castle in Strathspey, calling at Cawdor Castle on his way to Fort George and

Inverness. On his route to Aberdeen the poet stayed overnight with Brodie of Brodie in that famous castle, dining the following day with the Duke and Duchess of Gordon at their castle at Fochabers. He continued to Aberdeen via Montrose where he called on some of his relations.

Last visit to Edinburgh

From 29 November to 11 December 1791 Burns made his last visit to Edinburgh, staying about a week at the White Hart Inn in the Grassmarket. The old inn is still in the Grassmarket today, bearing the plaque above the archway for all to see that Burns stayed there.

Burns also visited Clarinda, who made an entry in her diary on 6 December 1831: 'This day I can never forget, I parted with Burns in the year 1791 never more to meet in this world. Oh, may we meet in Heaven.' On his return to Dumfries, Burns sent Clarinda 'Ae Fond Kiss'.

The poet left his lasting impression of Edinburgh through his poem 'Address to Edinburgh' (see p. 58) which he sent to his friend William Chalmers.

It is not surprising that after the poet's death a statue was eventually erected in Edinburgh to honour his memory, but it was surprising that the idea originated in Bombay, through a Mr John Forbes Hamilton. A meeting,

arranged by him with some of his close friends, was held in London in the Freemasons Tavern on 26 May 1821. Here it was agreed that funds amounting to about £1,500 would be available for a marble statue of Robert Burns. Thus in July 1824 an agreement was made with the celebrated sculptor John Flaxman, PSRA, to begin work on a life-size statue of Burns. (The sculptor used the oil-painting by Alexander Nasmyth to help him with his work.) When some doubt arose with regard to payment, the sculptor, to his credit and because of his admiration for the Scottish bard, proposed to complete his work with or without remuneration. Unfortunately, John Flaxman died before the completion of the statue. However, his pupil and brother-in-law, Joseph Denman, agreed to finish his work. A monument was later erected to house the statue and was placed in Regent Road, Edinburgh. Owing to the fear of deterioration and the fact that it was not easily accessible to the public, it was decided to remove the statue to the Scottish National Portrait Gallery in Queen Street, where it is on display today. This fine statue and the monument are under the care of the City of Edinburgh and District Council.

Above: An 18th-century engraving of the Grassmarket, Edinburgh

Left: Marble statue of Burns by John Flaxman

19

In St Giles Cathedral, Edinburgh, there is a magnificent stained glass window above the west door dedicated to the memory of Robert Burns. This work was designed by the Icelandic artist Leifur Breiðfjörð, who trained at the Edinburgh College of Art, and installed in 1985. The stained glass symbolises love, brotherhood of man, and nature – the very essence of Burns' poetical works.

Above: The Burns Memorial Window in St Giles Cathedral by Leifur Breiðfjörð
Below: Ellisland Farm *by Hunt*

Farming at Ellisland

Leaving Edinburgh behind, Robert Burns began another phase of his life in Dumfriesshire. He was not able to earn enough from his muse to live independently, so when he was offered a leasing of the small farm of Ellisland he felt he could not refuse. Although the poet had an uneasy feeling that the farm was not a viable proposition, he agreed to take the lease at a much reduced rent, and the landlord gave him financial assistance to enable him to build a new farmhouse, for there was no suitable dwelling at Ellisland.

Marriage to Jean Armour

Burns wanted to settle down, and with the prospects of the farm and a new home he again approached Jean Armour to join him at Ellisland. Their marriage took place in 1788 at Gavin Hamilton's, a Justice of the Peace and a personal friend of the poet. Hamilton was able to provide Burns with a certificate of marriage, which was officially recognised on 5 August 1788 by the Reverend William Auld and Mauchline Kirk Session. This finally satisfied Jean's father, although the original certificate given him by Burns had been a genuine marriage agreement. After a while they settled down in their new home at Ellisland. They were a devoted family, and both parents were very fond of their children.

It was while Burns was at Ellisland that he met, through his friend and next-door neighbour Robert Riddell of Friars Carse, the antiquarian Captain Francis Grose, who was in the process of collecting material for a book on the antiquities of Scotland. Burns wanted him to include an illustration

Right: Jean Armour (Mrs Burns) by J A Gilfillan (fl. 1830–40)

of the Auld Kirk at Alloway (see p. 62); but the wily Captain would only agree if Burns wrote a poem around it. And so it was that Burns composed, supposedly in one day, the most intriguing poetical story of Tam o' Shanter (see p. 60). Jean Burns relates how she saw Burns by the river laughing and gesticulating as the humorous incidents assumed shape in his mind.

Employment as an exciseman

During his years at Ellisland, Burns continued to write his verse and songs, but the farm was unremunerative, so it was just as well that the poet had already applied for employment as an excise officer when he was in Edinburgh. The farm after a time, as Burns suspected from the beginning, proved to be an ever-increasing burden. He wrote to his brother Gilbert, saying: 'I feel hypochondria pervading every atom of my body and soul. This farm has undone my enjoyment of myself. It is a ruinous affair on all hands.' His excise duties forced him to ride over 200 miles (320km) a week, and he was often ill in winter.

To Dumfries

It was not surprising that Burns finally decided to leave the farm for Dumfries and take up full-time employment as an excise officer. It was in late 1791 that Burns moved to a small house in Bank Street, then called 'The Wee Vennel'. His position as an excise officer was an exacting one, and he became fully occupied with it. Shortly before Burns came to Dumfries, the Old Town Mill house was erected beside the River Nith. This used to grind the town's corn and now houses the town's Robert Burns Centre, with an exhibition and audiovisual pro-gramme, paintings, manuscripts, books and artefacts connected with the poet and his life in Dumfries, including a model of the town in the 1790s.

In 1793 Burns moved to a larger house in Mill Brae Hole, now 'Burns House' in Burns Street. Here a museum displays many manuscripts and articles of interest associated with the poet.

Above left: Burns House, Burns Street, Dumfries
Above: Burns used this oak writing-desk when he visited Dr Jaffray and his daughter at the Old Manse, Lochmaben. During one visit he wrote 'The Blue-Eyed Lassie'. It is on exhibition at Burns House, Dumfries

During his Ellisland and Dumfries years, Burns devoted much time to song-writing. He loved researching and discovering the half-forgotten old Scottish songs and legends. He was not only able to unearth them but had the rare talent of giving them new life through the magic of his pen. He contributed 373 songs to James Johnson's *Scots Musical Museum* and

George Thomson's *Select Collection*. Burns was editor of the former in all but name.

Roots of Burns' genius

Many fine old Scottish tunes would have been lost but for Burns' putting words to them. The Scots all over the world have always kept their 'home fires burning' through their songs. Burns clearly appreciated this, but his brilliant song 'Auld Lang Syne' shows the depth of his desire for the brotherhood of man and commands a universal homage. Is it not a remarkable fact that whenever there is a festive occasion, particularly at New Year, no matter where you find yourself, those sterling words, as hands are clasped in parting, ring out their challenge to all?

Perhaps in a way, the very fact that Burns was obliged to labour long hours during his life had its own rewards. His closeness to nature gave him the opportunity for undisturbed observation, so when he could write his verse, he wrote what he had seen without embellishment. Maybe this was why his genius was so rare. The poet expresses so beautifully the

View over the River Nith in Dumfries

smallest creatures in nature, with such exactitude and grace in, for example, 'To a Mouse' and 'To a Louse' (see pp. 50 and 78).

There is a lovely story that tells us how Burns came to write 'To a Mouse'. He was ploughing the fields one day with John Blane, when a mouse's nest was unearthed. John Blane attacked it with his pattle (plough spade). Burns stopped him instantly, becoming quiet and remote for the rest of the day. Later, in the early hours of the morning, he awoke John Blane, handing him the poem 'To a Mouse'. 'Now,' said Burns, 'what do you think of the wee mouse?'

'Holy Willie's Prayer' (see p. 52) is another example of the poet's rare talent for expressing the truth as it is. This poem is said to be the 'most terrible commentary on the Calvinistic doctrine ever written'. Briefly, the poem relates how Burns' friend Gavin Hamilton, a Mauchline lawyer, had been refused the ordinance of the Church, because he was believed to have made a journey on the Sabbath, and because one of his servants, by his orders, had brought in some potatoes from the garden on another Sunday. Ironically, the very elder who had accused Hamilton was suspected of taking church funds and eventually died in a ditch in a helpless state of intoxication.

Sickness and death

By late 1795 Burns' health was causing concern. He was sent to Brow Well on the Solway Coast, a miserable spa with three cottages and a large tank. The mineral spring water was fed into the tank by a pipe. In spite of being a very sick man, Burns took the waters each day. On the advice of his doctors he also bathed in the sea, supposedly to relieve his rheumatism. The poet was unable to regain his former strength and returned home on 18 July 1796.

This circular silver snuff-box with decorated lid, inset with a Charles I crown coin, in a presentation case was given to Robert Burns by James Cunningham, 14th Earl of Glencairn, 25 January 1787. On exhibition at Burns House, Dumfries

Above: Burns Mausoleum, Dumfries
Bottom right: Robert Burns' signature

have said to his wife: 'Don't be afraid. I'll be more thought of a 100 years hence, than I am at present.' He died on 21 July 1796 in his 38th year, in his home at Mill Street, Dumfries. On 25 July he was buried with full military honours in St Michael's churchyard. The poet was a well-respected member of the Royal Dumfries Volunteers. Two regiments were in Dumfries at the time of his death, that of the Fencible Infantry of Angusshire and the Cinque Ports Cavalry; both were in attendance at Burns' funeral. In 1815 his remains were transferred to the elegant mausoleum erected in honour of his memory in the same churchyard.

In his short life, Burns became one of the greatest Scottish poets, gaining a worldwide reputation that is both remarkable and exceptional in every way. In a strange way, too, he immortalised himself by his own song 'Auld Lang Syne'. It would be hard to find another song with a greater appeal to highlight the festive celebrations of bringing in each New Year; or to find another poet who could touch the hearts of all men everywhere, so completely, through the magic of his verse.

He continually worried about the welfare of his wife and family, his wife was expecting their last child, which must have greatly added to his troubles. It is an extraordinary fact that today a first edition of Burns' poems would fetch a fortune, yet in Burns' day the poet received little remuneration for his masterpieces.

Unable to cope any longer with his ill health he was forced to his bed; he lingered only a few days. As he lay dying he is reported to

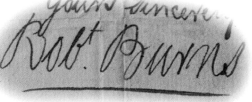

Robert Burns Country
and Heritage Trail

Map labels:

Johnstone
A78
M8
GLASGOW
M8
Paisley
Hamilton
Motherwell
Largs
East Kilbride
Larkhall
Millport
Burns Garden
Kilwinning
Burns Monument and Museum
Dean Castle
Newmilns
Dick Institute
Laigh and Old High kirks
Lanark
Ardrossan
Saltcoats
Eglinton Woods
Darvel
M74
A73
Glasgow Vennel, Irvine
Irvine Burns Club Museum
Irvine
Kilmarnock
Greenholm
Galston
Mauchline kirkyard
Poosie Nansie's Tavern
Troon
A77
Tarbolton
Castle Montgomery
Bachelors' Club
Prestwick
Mauchline
Ayr
Failford
Burns House Museum
Burns Memorial Tower
A74(M)
Auld Brig
Auld Kirk
Holmhead
Alloway Kirk
Burns Monument
Brig o' Doon
Tam o' Shanter Experience
Culzean Castle
Alloway
Burns Cottage
Cumnock
Highland Mary's Monument
Leglen Wood
New Cumnock
Afton Water
River Nith
Sanquhar
ilsa Craig
Maybole
Kirkoswald
River Doon
A719
Kirkoswald churchyard
Souter Johnnie's Cottage
Girvan
Loch Doon
A713
DUMFRIES AN
Ellis
Glo
Bu
B734
Dee
River
A702
Loch Urr
A77
A714
River Cree
Clatteringshaws Loch
New Galloway
A712
A713
Urr Water
Dum
Cairnryan
A718
Water of Luce
A712
A762
Castle Douglas
Glencapl
Stranraer
A75
Newton Stewart
B796
Loch Ken
Dalbeattie
A710
Wigtown
A747
A746
Gatehouse of Fleet
A75
Kirkcudbright
A711
Solway
Murray Arms Hotel
Luce Bay
Whithorn
Wigtown Bay
Selkirk Arms Hotel
Ma
Workingto
Whitehaven

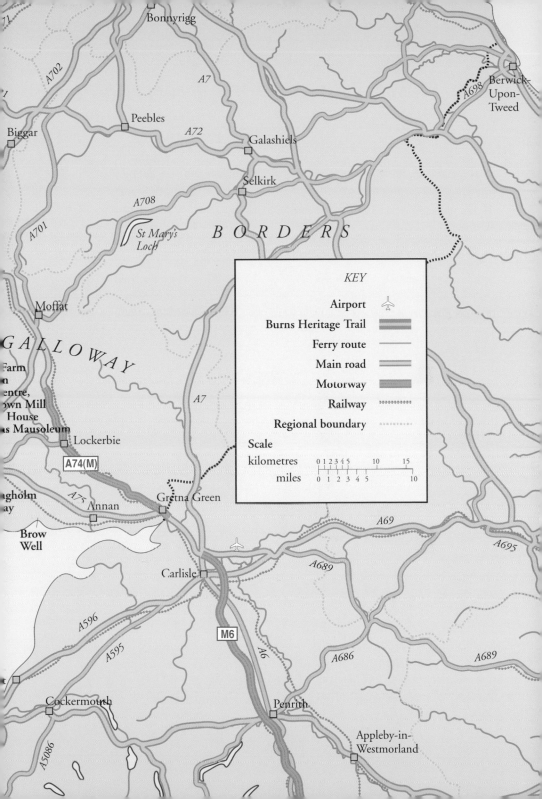

Bonnyrigg

A702

A7

A698 Berwick-Upon-Tweed

Biggar

Peebles

A72

Galashiels

Selkirk

A708

St Mary's Loch

B O R D E R S

A701

Moffat

G A L L O W A Y

A7

KEY

Airport ✈

Burns Heritage Trail

Ferry route

Main road

Motorway

Railway

Regional boundary

Scale
kilometres
miles

0 1 2 3 4 5   10   15

0 1 2 3 4 5   10

Farm
n
entre,
wn Mill
House
s Mausoleum

Lockerbie

A74(M)

A75

gholm
ay

Annan

Brow
Well

Gretna Green

A69

A695

Carlisle

A689

A596

A595

M6

A6

A686

A689

Cockermouth

Penrith

A5086

Appleby-in-Westmorland

The Robert Burns World Federation Ltd

O n 7 March 1885 the bust of Robert Burns was unveiled in Poets' Corner in Westminster Abbey, London. Afterwards, Provost David Mackay and Captain Sneddon, both from Kilmarnock, along with Colin Rae Brown, President of London Burns Club, were walking along the Thames Embankment, when Provost Mackay remarked that it would be good to establish a federation of Burns clubs and societies throughout the world.

The idea appealed to his companions so a meeting was called and held in Kilmarnock in 17 July 1885.

From this seed of inspiration grew an organisation recognised worldwide as the custodian of the works and philosophies of Robert Burns.

The Burns Federation has been successful over the years in maintaining interest in Scottish literature, especially in Scottish schools where annually around 170,000 pupils take part in competitions celebrating their culture.

Instituted 1892

The future of any organisation depends on its youth, and we are delighted to have School Burns Clubs within our membership. We are anxious that they feel part of the wider Burns Movement, and many take an active part in the annual conference held each year in different parts of the country, as well as overseas.

Monuments and memorials associated with the poet are a permanent and tangible reminder of Burns and his associates, with their upkeep supported by the Federation through its local Burns Clubs.

The presence of the Burns Heritage Trail indicates the importance afforded to our National Bard.

The Burns Federation plays a vital part in the continuing publicity around the 25 January, the anniversary of Robert Burns' birth. Help is given in the co-ordination of Burns Suppers, which are a growing phenomenon. The last estimate was that around half a million Burns

Suppers take place throughout the world annually.

The official publication of the Federation is the *Burns Chronicle*, which provides academics and members with the opportunity of communicating their thoughts and activities to a worldwide audience.

The Burns Federation is believed to be the oldest literary society in Scotland – and has served its members well for many years. However, in 1997 it was recognised that change had to take place to further its aims and objectives. To this end a momentous decision was taken at the Conference of the Council on 12 September 1998. Delegates voted to accept the promotion and incorporation of a company limited by guarantee. The company would have full charitable status and be named 'The Robert Burns World Federation Ltd'.

The running of the company is in the hands of a Board of Directors elected by the membership. Committees with varying tasks promote the aims and objectives, which are:

To advance the education of the public, without distinction of sex or of political or religious opinions about the life, poetry and works of Robert Burns and in furtherance thereof:
1. to encourage and arrange competitions among the general public, students and/or schoolchildren to stimulate the teaching and studying of Scottish literature, history, art, music and language
2. to stimulate the development of Scottish literature, art, music and language
3. to conserve buildings and places associated with Robert Burns and his contemporaries, and
4. to strengthen the bond of the fellowship amongst members of Burns Clubs and kindred societies to honour the memory of Robert Burns and his works
5. to promote, encourage and undertake experimental work or conduct research consistent with the objects of the company, publishing or making available, whether gratuitously or otherwise, the useful results of such research
6. to research, maintain and extend genealogical records in relation to the Burns family.

The new company will continue to further the aims of the Burns Federation through a streamlined structure, active membership and with adequate resources to achieve its objectives.

The Robert Burns World Federation Ltd is happy to welcome new members dedicated to keeping alive the rich literary heritage, traditions and culture associated with Scotland.

Shirley Bell, Chief Executive
The Robert Burns World Federation Ltd
Dick Institute, Elmbank Avenue
Kilmarnock KA1 3BU
Tel. 01563 572469; Fax 01563 529661
E-mail: RobertBurnsFederation
@kilmarnock26.freeserve.co.uk

Scots, Wha Hae

'There is a tradition,' says Burns, in a letter to George Thomson, 'that the old air "Hey, Tuttie Taitie" was Robert Bruce's March at the Battle of Bannockburn (1314). This thought in my solitary wanderings has warmed me to a pitch of enthusiasm; as the theme of liberty and independence which I have thrown into a kind of Scottish ode. Fitted to the air that one might suppose to be the gallant Scot's address to his heroic followers on that eventful morning.'

wha hae – *who have*

aften – *often*

Scots, wha hae wi Wallace bled,
Scots, wham Bruce has aften led,
Welcome to your gory bed
    Or to victorie!

Now's the day, and now's the hour:
See the front o battle lour,
See approach proud Edward's power –
    Chains and slaverie!

Wha will be a traitor knave?
    Wha can fill a coward's grave?
Wha sae base as be a slave? –
    Let him turn, and flee!

Wha for Scotland's King and Law
Freedom's sword will strongly draw,
Freeman stand, or Freeman fa',
    Let him follow me!

By Oppression's woes and pains,
By your sons in servile chains,
We will drain our dearest veins,
    But they shall be free!

Lay the proud usurpers low!
Tyrants fall in every foe!
Liberty's in every blow! –
    Let us do, or die!

Opposite: The statue of Robert Bruce
(1274–1329) at Bannockburn

A Man's a Man for A' That

Burns said of this song: 'A great critic on songs says that love and wine are the two exclusive schemes for song writing. The following is on neither subject.'

hings – *hangs*
gowd – *gold*
hoddin grey –
*coarse undyed
woollen cloth*
hamely – *homely*
birkie – *fellow*
coof – *fool*
aboon – *above*
mauna fa' that –
must not fail

bear the gree –
have priority

Is there for honest poverty
    That hings his head, an a' that?
The coward slave, we pass him by –
    We dare be poor for a' that!
For a' that, an a' that,
    Our toils obscure, an a' that,
The rank is but the guinea's stamp,
    The man's the gowd for a' that.

What though on hamely fare we dine,
    Wear hoddin grey, an a' that?
Gie fools their silks, and knaves their wine –
    A man's a man for a' that.
For a' that, an a' that,
    Their tinsel show, an a' that,
The honest man, tho e'er sae poor,
    Is king o men for a' that.

Ye see yon birkie ca'd 'a lord',
    Wha struts, an stares, and a' that?
Though hundreds worship at his word,
    He's but a coof for a' that.
For a' that, an a' that,
    His ribband, star, an a' that,
The man of independent mind,
    He looks an laughs at a' that.

A prince can mak a belted knight,
    A marquis, duke, an a' that!
But an honest man's aboon his might –
    Guid faith, he mauna fa' that!
For a' that, an a' that,
    Their dignities, an a' that,
The pith o sense, an pride o worth,
    Are higher rank than a' that.

Then let us pray that come it may
   (As come it will for a' that),
That Sense and Worth o'er a' the earth,
   Shall bear the gree an a' that.
For a' that, an a' that,
   It's comin yet for a' that,
That man to man, the warld, o'er
   Shall brithers be for a' that.

*The mural at Irvine
Burns Museum depicts
scenes from Burns' life*

34

Ae Fond Kiss

Ae fond kiss, and then we sever!
Ae farewell, and then forever!
Deep in heart-wrung tears I'll pledge thee,
Warring sighs and groans I'll wage thee.
Who shall say that Fortune grieves him,
While the star of hope she leaves him?
Me, nae cheerfu twinkle lights me,
Dark despair around benights me.

I'll ne'er blame my partial fancy:
Naething could resist my Nancy!
But to see her was to love her,
Love but her, and love for ever.
Had we never lov'd sae kindly,
Had we never lov'd sae blindly,
Never met – or never parted –
We had ne'er been broken-hearted.

Fare-thee-weel, thou first and fairest!
Fare-thee-weel, thou best and dearest!
Thine be ilka joy and treasure,
Peace, Enjoyment, Love and Pleasure!
Ae fond kiss, and then we sever!
Ae farewell, alas, for ever!
Deep in heart-wrung tears I'll pledge thee,
Warring sighs and groans I'll wage thee.

Burns dedicated this poem to 'Nancy' Maclehose (Clarinda). It is reputed to be one of the greatest love-songs ever written

nae – *not*
ilka – *every*

Opposite: Silhouette on plaster of 'Clarinda' (Mrs Agnes 'Nancy' Maclehose, 1759–1841) by John Miers, 1788

Ca' the Yowes to the Knowes

Hark, the mavis e'ening sang
Sounding Clouden's woods amang
Then a-faulding let us gang,
    My bonie dearie.

Chorus
Ca' the yowes to the knowes,
Ca' them where the heather grows,
Ca' them where the burnie rowes,
    My bonie dearie.

We'll gae down by Clouden side,
Thro the hazels, spreading wide
O'er the waves that sweetly glide
    To the moon sae clearly.

Yonder Clouden's silent towers
Where, at moonshine's midnight hours,
O'er the dewy bending flowers
    Fairies dance sae cheery.

Ghaist nor bogle shalt thou fear –
Thou'rt to Love and Heav'n sae dear
Nocht of ill may come thee near,
    My bonie dearie.

*A shepherd and his dog
from Eskdalemuir,
Dumfries and
Galloway*

Bonie Wee Thing

Wishfully I look and languish
    In that bonie face o thine,
And my heart it stounds wi anguish,
    Lest my wee thing be na mine.

Chorus
Bonie wee thing, cannie wee thing,
    Lovely wee thing, wert thou mine,
I wad wear thee in my bosom
    Lest my jewel I should tine.

Wit and Grace and Love and Beauty
    In ae constellation shine!
To adore thee is my duty,
    Goddess o this soul o mine!

wee – *little*
na – *not*
cannie – *gentle*
tine – *lose*
stounds – *throbs*

*Loch Trool, Dumfries
and Galloway*

O, Whistle an I'll Come to Ye, My Lad!

gae – *go*

tent – *take care*

yett – *gate*

a-jee – *ajar*

syne – *then*

flie – *fly*

blink – *glance*

whyles – *sometimes*

lightly – *disparage*

a-wee – *a little*

wyle – *lure*

But warily tent when ye come to court me,
And come nae unless the back-yett be a-jee;
Syne up the back-style, and let naebody see,
And come as ye were na comin to me,
And come as ye were na comin to me!

Chorus
O, whistle an I'll come to ye, my lad!
O, whistle an I'll come to ye, my lad!
Tho father an mother an a should gae mad,
O, whistle an I'll come to ye, my lad!

At kirk, or at market, whene'er ye meet me,
Gang by me as tho that ye car'd na a flie;
But steal me a blink o your bonie black e'e,
Yet look as ye were na lookin to me,
Yet look as ye were na lookin to me!

Ay vow and protest that ye care na for me,
And whyles ye may lightly my beauty a-wee;
But court nae anither tho jokin ye be,
For fear that she wyle your fancy frae me,
For fear that she wyle your fancy frae me!

*Opposite: Lady Stair's
House, Edinburgh*

Afton Water

Flow gently, sweet Afton, among thy green braes!
Flow gently, I'll sing thee a song in they praise!
My Mary's asleep by thy murmuring stream –
Flow gently, sweet Afton, disturb not her dream!

Thou stock dove whose echo resounds thro the glen,
Ye wild whistling blackbirds in yon thorny den,
Thou green-crested lapwing, thy screaming forbear –
I charge you, disturb not my slumbering Fair.

How lofty, sweet Afton, thy neighbouring hills,
Far mark'd with the courses of clear, winding rills!
There daily I wander, as noon rise high,
My flocks and my Mary's sweet cot in my eye.

How pleasant thy banks and green vallies below,
Where wild in the woodlands the primroses blow
There oft, as mild Ev'ning weeps over the lea,
The sweet-scented birk shades my Mary and me.

Thy crystal stream, Afton, how lovely it glides,
And winds by the cot where my Mary resides!
How wanton thy waters her snowy feet lave,
As, gathering sweet flowerets, she stems thy clear wave!

Flow gently, sweet Afton, among thy green braes!
Flow gently, sweet river, the theme of my lays!
My Mary's asleep by thy murmuring stream –
Flow gently, sweet Afton, disturb not her dream!

Gilbert Burns affirms he heard his brother say that this song, also known as 'Sweet Afton', was a tribute to his dearly loved Highland Mary

braes – *slopes*
birk – *birch*
lave – *wash*

Opposite: Glen Afton, south of New Cumnock, East Ayrshire

The Gloomy Night is Gath'ring Fast

The gloomy night is gath'ring fast,
Loud roars the wild inconstant blast;
Yon murky cloud is foul with rain,
I see it driving o'er the plain;
The hunter now has left the moor,
The scatt'red coveys meet secure;
While here I wander, prest with care,
Along the lonely banks of Ayr.

The Autumn mourns her rip'ning corn
By early Winter's ravage torn;
Across her placid, azure sky,
She sees the scowling tempest fly;
Chill runs my blood to hear it rave;
I think upon the stormy wave,
Where many a danger I must dare,
Far from the bonie banks of Ayr.

'Tis not the surging billows' roar,
'Tis not that fatal, deadly shore;
Tho death in ev'ry shape appear,
The wretched have no more to fear:
But round my heart the ties are bound,
The heart transpierc'd with many a wound;
These bleed afresh, those ties I tear,
To leave the bonie banks of Ayr.

Farewell, old Coila's hills and dales,
Her heathy moors and winding vales;
The scenes where wretched Fancy roves,
Pursuing past unhappy loves!
Farewell my friends! farewell my foes!
My peace with these, my love with those –
The bursting tears my heart declare,
Farewell, the bonie banks of Ayr!

As the stanzas opposite, this song was composed when Burns had made plans to give up farming and emigrate to Jamaica

Above: The Auld Brig in the town of Ayr

The Farewell

Farewell, old Scotia's bleak domains,
Far dearer than the torrid plains,
   Where rich ananas blow!
Farewell, a mother's blessing dear
A brother's sigh, a sister's tear,
   My Jean's heart-rending throe!
Farewell, my Bess! Tho thou'rt bereft
   Of my parental care,
A faithful brother I have left,
   My part in him thou'lt share!
     Adieu too, to you too,
       My Smith, my bosom frien';
     When kindly you mind me,
       O, then befriend my Jean!

What bursting anguish tears my heart?
From thee, my Jeany, must I part?
   Thou, weeping, answ'rest – 'No!'
Alas! misfortune stares my face,
And points to ruin and disgrace –
   I for they sake must go!
Thee, Hamilton, and Aiken dear,
   A grateful, warm adieu:
I with a much-indebted tear
   Shall still remember you!
     All-hail then, the gale then –
       Wafts me from thee, dear shore!
     It rustles and whistles –
       I'll never see thee more!

'The following touching stanzas,' says Cunningham, 'were composed in the autumn of 1786, when the prospects of the poet darkened, and he looked towards the West Indies as a place of refuge, and perhaps of hope. All who share his affections are mentioned – but in nothing he ever wrote was his affection for Jean Armour more tenderly or more naturally displayed.'

ananas –
pineapples

My Heart's in the Highlands

The refrain of this song is old, the rest is Burns' own

Farewell to the Highlands, farewell to the North,
The birthplace of valour, the country of worth!
Wherever I wander, wherever I rove,
The hills of the Highlands for ever I love.

Chorus
My heart's in the Highlands, my heart is not here
My heart's in the Highlands, a-chasing the deer,
A-chasing the wild deer, and following the roe –
My heart's in the Highlands, wherever I go!

Farewell to the mountains, high-cover'd with snow,
Farewell to the straths and green valleys below,
Farewell to the forests and wild-hanging woods,
Farewell to the torrents and loud-pouring floods!

Below: A red deer
Opposite: Beinn Dearg
Waterfall, Glen Torridon

My Father was a Farmer

My father was a farmer
    upon the Carrick border, O,
And carefully he bred me
    in decency and order, O,
He bade me act a manly part,
    though I had ne'er a farthing, O,
For without an honest manly heart,
    no man was worth regarding, O.

Then out into the world
    my course I did determine, O,
Tho to be rich was not my wish,
    yet to be great was charming, O.
My talents they were not the worst,
    nor yet my education, O,
Resolv'd was I, at least to try,
    to mend my situation, O.

Lochlea Farm, Tarbolton (anon), where Robert Burns' father, William Burnes, died on 13 February 1784

In many a way, and vain essay,
　　I courted Fortune's favour, O:
Some cause unseen still stept between,
　　to frustrate each endeavour, O.
Sometimes by foes I was o'erpower'd,
　　sometimes by friends forsaken, O,
And when my hope was at the top,
　　I still was worst mistaken, O.

Then sore harass'd, and tir'd at last,
　　with Fortune's vain delusion, O,
I dropt my schemes, like idle dreams,
　　and came to this conclusion, O –
The past was bad, and the future hid,
　　its good or ill untried, O,
But the present hour was in my pow'r,
　　and so I would enjoy it, O.

No help, nor hope, nor view had I,
　　nor person to befriend me, O,
So I must toil, and sweat, and moil,
　　and labour to sustain me, O.
To plough and sow, to reap and mow,
　　my father bred me early, O;
For one, he said, to labour bred,
　　was a match for Fortune fairly, O.

Thus all obscure, unknown, and poor,
　　thro life I'm doom'd to wander, O,
Till down my weary bones I lay
　　in everlasting slumber, O.
No view nor care, but shun whate'er
　　might breed me pain or sorrow, O,
I live to-day as well's I may,
　　regardless of to-morrow, O.

But cheerful still, I am as well
　　as a monarch in a palace, O,
Tho Fortune's frown still hunts me down,
　　with all her wonted malice, O:
I make indeed may daily bread,
　　but ne'er can make it farther, O,
But, as daily bread is all I need,
　　I do not much regard her, O.

When sometime by my labour,
　　I earn a little money, O,
Some unforeseen misfortune
　　comes gen'rally upon me, O;
Mischance, mistake, or by neglect,
　　or my good-natur'd folly, O:
But, come what will, I've sworn it still,
　　I'll ne'er be melancholy, O.

All you who follow wealth and power
　　with unremitting ardour, O,
The more in this you look for bliss,
　　you leave your view the farther, O,
Had you the wealth Potosi boasts,
　　or nations to adore you, O,
A cheerful honest-hearted clown
　　I will prefer before you, O.

The Cotter's Saturday Night

Burns says:
'The cotter, in the
Saturday Night, is
an exact copy of
my father in his
manners, his
family devotion,
and exhortations;
yet the other parts
of the description
do not apply to
my family.'
 The poem
was inscribed to
Robert Aiken
(1739-1807)
over the winter
of 1785-6

halesome parritch
– *wholesome*
porridge

soupe – *milk*

hawkie – *cow*

'yont the hallan –
beyond the
partition

well-hain'd
kebbuck – *well-*
saved cheese,
strong

Selected verses

My lov'd, my honour'd, much-respected friend!
 No mercenary bard his homage pays;
With honest pride, I scorn each selfish end,
 My dearest meed, a friend's esteem and praise:
 To you I sing, in simple Scottish lays,
The lowly train in life's sequester'd scene;
 The native feelings strong, the guileless ways;
What Aiken in a cottage would have been;
Ah! tho his worth unknown, far happier there, I ween!

But now the supper crowns their simple board,
 The halesome parritch, chief o Scotia's food;
The soupe their only hawkie does afford,
 That, 'yont the hallan snugly chows her cood:
 The dame brings forth, in complimental mood,
To grace the lad, her weel-hain'd kebbuck, fell;
 And aft he's prest, and aft he ca's it guid:
The frugal wifie, garrulous, will tell,
How 'twas a towmond auld, sin lint was i' the bell.

From scenes like these, old Scotia's grandeur springs,
 That makes her lov'd at home, rever'd abroad:
Princes and lords are but the breath of kings,
 'An honest man's the noblest work of God';
 And certes, in fair Virtue's heavenly road,
The cottage leaves the palace far behind;
 What is a lordling's pomp? a cumbrous load,
Disguising oft the wretch of human kind,
Studied in arts of Hell, in wickedness refin'd!

O Scotia! my dear, my native soil!
    For whom my warmest wish to Heaven is sent!
Long may thy hardy sons of rustic toil
    Be blest with health, and peace, and sweet content!
    And O! may Heaven their simple lives prevent
From Luxury's contagion, weak and vile!
    Then, howe'er crowns and coronets be rent,
A virtuous populace may rise the while,
And stand a wall of fire around their much-lov'd Isle.

O Thou! who pour'd the patriotic tide,
    That stream'd thro Wallace's undaunted heart,
Who dar'd to, nobly, stem tyrannic pride,
    Or nobly die, the second glorious part:
    (The patriot's God, peculiarly Thou art,
His friend, inspirer, guardian, and reward!)
    O never, never Scotia's realm desert;
But still the patriot, and the patriot-bard
In bright succession raise, her ornament and guard!

towmond – *twelve month*

lint – *flax*

bell – *flower*

Original manuscript of 'The Cotter's Saturday Night'

To a Mouse

Above: An engraving of Burns turning up the mouse from her nest with the plough in November 1785. However, he ploughed with four horses, never two, the horses were smaller and the ground largely undrained and heavy – also, Burns would not have ploughed in his Sunday best!

Wee sleekit, cow'rin, tim'rous beastie,
O, what a panic's in thy breastie!
Thou need na start awa' sae hasty,
 Wi bickering brattle!
I wad be laith to rin an chase thee,
 Wi murdering pattle!

I'm truly sorry man's dominion
Has broken Nature's social union,
An justifies that ill opinion,
 Which makes thee startle
At me, thy poor, earth-born companion,
 An fellow-mortal!

I doubt na, whyles, but thou may thieve;
What then? poor beastie, thou maun live!
A daimen icker in a thrave
 'S a sma request:
I'll get a blessin wi the lave,
 An never miss't!

Thy wee-bit housie, too, in ruin!
Its silly wa's the win's are strewin!
And naething, now, to big a new ane,
 O foggage green!
An bleak December's wind's ensuin,
 Baith snell an keen!

Thou saw the fields laid bare an waste,
An weary winter comin fast,
An cozie here, beneath the blast,
 Thou thought to dwell,
Till crash! the cruel coulter past
 Out thro thy cell.

That wee-bit heap o leaves an stibble,
Has cost thee monie a' weary nibble!
Now thou's turn'd out for a thy trouble,
 But house or hald,
To thole the winter's sleety dribble,
 An cranreuch cauld!

But, Mousie, thou art no thy lane,
In proving foresight may be vain:
The best-laid schemes o mice an men
 Gang aft agley,
An lea'e us nought but grief an pain,
 For promis'd joy!

Still thou art blest, compar'd wi me!
The present only toucheth thee:
But och! I backward cast my e'e,
 On prospects drear!
An forward, tho I canna see,
 I guess an fear!

strewin – *scatter*

big – *build*

foggage – *foliage*

snell – *bitter*

coulter – *plough-share*

but – *without*

hald – *holding*

thole – *endure*

cranreuch – *hoar-frost*

no thy lane – *not alone*

gang aft agley – *go often awry*

Holy Willie's Prayer

sic – *such*

gooms – *gums*

buckler – *shield*

Selected verses

O Thou that in the Heavens does dwell,
Wha, as it pleases best Thysel,
Sends ane to Heaven, and ten to Hell,
　　A' for Thy glory,
And no for onie guid or ill
　　They've done before Thee!

I bless and praise Thy matchless might,
When thousands Thou hast left in night,
That I am here before Thy sight,
　　For gifts and grace,
A burning and a shining light
　　To a' this place.

What was I, or my generation,
That I should get sic exaltation?
I, wha deserv'd most just damnation
　　For broken laws,
Sax thousand years ere my creation,
　　Thro Adam's cause!

When from my mother's womb I fell,
Thou might hae plung'd me deep in Hell,
To gnash my gooms, and weep and wail,
　　In burning lakes,
Whare damned devils roar and yell,
　　Chain'd to their stakes.

Yet I am here a chosen sample,
To show Thy grace is great and ample:
I'm here a pillar o Thy temple,
　　Strong as a rock,
A guide, a buckler, and example,
　　To a' Thy flock!

But yet, O Lord! confess I must,
At times I'm fash'd wi fleshly lust;
And sometimes, too, in warldly trust,
    Vile self gets in;
But Thou remembers we are dust,
    Defil'd wi sin.

O Lord! yestreen, Thou kens, wi Meg
Thy pardon I sincerely beg –
O, may't ne'er be a living plague
    To my dishonour!
And I'll ne'er lift a lawless leg
    Again upon her.

Besides, I farther maun avow,
Wi Leezie's lass, three times I trow –
But, Lord, that Friday I was fou,
    When I cam near her,
Or else, Thou kens, Thy servant true
    Wad never steer her.

fash'd – *irked*

splore – *disturbance*

yestreen – *last night*

maun – *must*

fou – *drunk*

steer – *meddle with*

Above: The Queen's View over Loch Tummel, Perth and Kinross

splore – *row*

dinna – *do not*

Maybe Thou lets this fleshly thorn
Buffet Thy servant e'en and morn,
Lest he owre proud and high should turn,
    That he's sae gifted:
If sae, Thy han' maun e'en be borne,
    Until Thou lift it.

Lord, bless Thy chosen in this place,
For here Thou hast a chosen race!
But God confound their stubborn face,
    And blast their name,
Wha bring Thy elders to disgrace
    And public shame.

Lord, mind Gau'n Hamilton's deserts:
He drinks, and swears, and play at cartes,
Yet has sae monie takin arts,
    Wi great and sma',
Frae God's ain Priest the people's hearts
    He steals awa.

And when we chasten'd him therefore,
Thou kens how he bred sic a splore,
And set the warld in a roar
    O laughin at us;
Curse Thou his basket and his store,
    Kail and potatoes!

Lord, hear my earnest cry and pray'r,
Against the Presbyt'ry o Ayr!
Thy strong right hand, Lord, mak it bare
    Upo' their heads!
Lord, visit them, and dinna spare,
    For their misdeeds!

Epitaph on Holy Willie

sair – *very, sore*

saul – *soul*

grun – *ground*

brunstane – *brim-stone*

haud – *hold back*

ance – *once*

coof – *fool*

Here Holy Willie's sair worn clay
    Taks up its last abode;
His saul has ta'en some other way –
    I fear, the left-hand road.

Stop! there he is as sure's a gun!
    Poor, silly body, see him!
Nae wonder he's as black's the grun –
    Observe wha's standing wi him!

Your brunstane Devilship, I see,
    Has got him there before ye!
But haud your nine-tail cat a wee,
    Till ance you've heard my story.

Your pity I will not implore,
    For pity ye have nane.
Justice, alas! has gi'en him o'er,
    And mercy's day is gane.

But hear me, Sir, Deil as ye are,
    Look something to your credit:
A coof like him wad stain your name,
    If it were kent ye did it!

*Above: The River Tay
at Dunkeld, Perth
and Kinross*

Epistle to Davie, a Brother Poet

hing us owre the
ingle – *double us
up over the fire*

westlin – *western*

Ben to the chimla
lug – *Right to the
chimney corner*

bien – *prosperous*

tent – *value*

chiels – *fellows*

coofs – *fools*

fash – *trouble*

gear – *goods/
wealth*

hale and fier –
whole and sound

*David Sillar
(1760–1830), like
Burns, was a
member of the
Tarbolton
Bachelors' Club*

Selected verses

While winds frae aff Ben Lomond blaw,
And bar the doors wi drivin snaw,
    And hing as owre the ingle,
I set me down to pass the time,
And spin a verse or twa o rhyme,
    In hamely, westlin jingle:
While frosty winds blaw in the drift,
    Ben to the chimla lug,
I grudge a wee the great-folk's gift,
That live sae bien an snug:
    I tent less, and want less
      Their roomy fire-side;
    But hanker, and canker,
      To see their cursed pride.

It's hardly in a body's pow'r,
To keep, at times, frae being sour,
    To see how things are shar'd;
How best o chiels are whyles in want,
While coofs on countless thousands rant,
    And ken na how to ware't;
But, Davie*, lad, ne'er fash your head
    Tho we hae little gear;
We're fit to win our daily bread,
    As lang's we're hale and fier:
    'Mair spier na, nor fear na,'
      Auld age ne'er mind a feg;
    The last o't, the warst o't,
      Is only but to beg.

It's no in titles nor in rank:
It's no in wealth like Lon'on Bank,
    To purchase peace and rest,
It's no in makin muckle, mair;
It's no in books, it's no in lear,
    To make us truly blest:
If happiness hae not her seat
    An centre in the breast,
We may be wise, or rich, or great,
    But never can be blest!
    Nae treasures nor pleasures
      Could make us happy lang;
    The heart ay's the part ay
      That makes us right or wrang.

muckle, mair –
much, more

Ben Lomond

Address to Edinburgh

Burns, when writing to his friend William Chalmers, sent him the following poem

*Eliza Burnett, Lord Monboddo's youngest daughter

Edina! Scotia's darling seat!
    All hail thy palaces and tow'rs,
Where once beneath a Monarch's feet,
    Sat Legislation's sov'reign pow'rs:
From marking wildly-scatt'red flow'rs,
    As on the banks of Ayr I stray'd,
And singing, lone, the ling'ring hours,
    I shelter in thy honor'd shade.

Here Wealth still swells the golden tide,
    As busy Trade his labour plies;
There Architecture's noble pride
    Bids elegance and splendour rise:
Here Justice, from her native skies,
    High wields her balance and her rod;
There Learning, with his eagle eyes,
    Seeks Science in her coy abode.

Thy sons, Edina, social, kind,
    With open arms the stranger hail;
Their views enlarg'd, their lib'ral mind,
    Above the narrow, rural vale;
Attentive still to Sorrow's wail,
    Or modest Merit's silent claim:
And never may their sources fail!
    And never Envy blot their name!

Thy daughters bright thy walks adorn,
    Gay as the gilded summer sky,
Sweet as the dewy, milk-white thorn,
    Dear as the raptur'd thrill of joy!
Fair Burnet* strikes th' adoring eye,
    Heav'n's beauties on my fancy shine:
I see the Sire of Love on high,
    And own His work indeed divine!

There, watching high the least alarms,
  Thy rough, rude fortress gleams afar;
Like some bold vet'ran, grey in arms,
  And mark'd with many a seamy scar:
The pond'rous wall and massy bar,
  Grim-rising o'er the rugged rock,
Have oft withstood assailing war,
  And oft repell'd the invader's shock.

With awe-struck thought and pitying tears,
  I view that noble, stately dome,
Where Scotia's kings of other years,
  Fam'd heroes! had their royal home:
Alas, how chang'd the times to come!
  Their royal name low in the dust!
Their hapless race wild-wand'ring roam!
  Tho rigid Law cries out, 'Twas just!'

*An 18th-century
engraving of Canongate
Tolbooth, Edinburgh*

Wild beats my heart to trace your steps,
  Whose ancestors, in days of yore,
Thro hostile ranks and ruin'd gaps
  Old Scotia's bloody lion bore:
Ev'n I, who sing in rustic lore,
  Haply my sires have left their shed,
And fac'd grim Danger's loudest roar,
  Bold-following where your fathers led!

Edina! Scotia's darling seat!
  All hail thy palaces and tow'rs,
Where once beneath a Monarch's feet,
  Sat Legislation's sov'reign pow'rs:
From marking wildly scatt'red flow'rs,
  As on the banks of Ayr I stray'd,
And singing, lone, the ling'ring hours,
  I shelter in thy honor'd shade.

Tam o Shanter

chapman billies – *pedlars*
drouthy – *thirsty*
gate – *road*
nappy – *ale*
fou – *drunk*
unco – *uncommon(ly)*
slaps – *pools*
styles – *openings*
fand – *found*
ae – *one*
taen – *(to have) taken*
skellum – *good-for-nothing*
blethering – *chattering*
blellum – *babbler*
ilka melder – *every meal-grinding*
siller – *money*
naig – *nag*
mirk – *dark*

When chapman billies leave the street,
And drouthy neibors, neibors meet;
As market-days are wearing late,
And folk begin to tak the gate;
While we sit bousing at the nappy,
And getting fou and unco happy,
We think na on the lang Scots miles,
The mosses, waters, slaps, and styles,
That lie between us and our hame,
Whare sits our sulky, sullen dame,
Gathering her brows like gathering storm,
Nursing her wrath to keep it warm.

This truth fand honest Tam o Shanter,
As he frae Ayr ae night did canter:
(Auld Ayr, whom ne'er a town surpasses,
For honest men and bonie lasses).

O, Tam, hadst thou but been sae wise,
As taen thy ain wife Kate's advice!
She tauld thee weel thou was a skellum,
A blethering, blustering, drunken blellum;
That frae November till October,
Ae market-day thou was nae sober;
That ilka melder wi the miller,
Thou sat as lang as thou had siller;
That ev'ry naig was ca'd a shoe on,
The smith and thee gat roarin fou on;
That at the Lord's house, even on Sunday,
Thou drank wi Kirkton Jean till Monday.
She prophesied that, late or soon,
Thou would be found, deep drown'd in Doon;
Or catch'd wi warlocks in the mirk,
By Alloway's auld, haunted kirk.

Ah, gentle dames, it gars me greet,
To think how monie counsels sweet,
How monie lengthen'd, sage advices
The husband frae the wife despises!

But to our tale: – Ae market night,
Tam had got planted unco right,
Fast by an ingle, bleezing finely,
Wi reaming swats, that drank divinely;
And at his elbow, Souter Johnie,
His ancient, trusty, drouthy cronie:
Tam lo'ed him like a very brither;
They had been fou for weeks thegither.
The night drave on wi sangs and clatter;

*Statue of Tam o' Shanter
by James Thom*

rair – *roar*
lades – *loads*
maun – *must*
sic – *such*
'twad blawn – *it
would have blown*

*Above: The Auld Kirk
at Alloway, 'Whare
ghaists and houlets
nightly cry'*

And ay the ale was growing better:
The landlady and Tam grew gracious,
Wi secret favours, sweet and precious:
The Souter tauld his queerest stories;
The landlord's laugh was ready chorus:
The storm without might rair and rustle,
Tam did na mind the storm a whistle.

    Care, mad to see a man sae happy,
E'en drown'd himsel amang the nappy.
As bees flee hame wi lades o treasure,
The minutes wing'd their way wi pleasure:
Kings may be blest but Tam was glorious,
O'er a' the ills o life victorious!

    But pleasures are like poppies spread:
You seize the flow'r, its bloom is shed;
Or like the snow falls in the river,
A moment white – then melts for ever;
Or like the borealis race,
That flit ere you can point their place;
Or like the rainbow's lovely form
Evanishing amid the storm.
Nae man can tether time or tide,
The hour approaches Tam maun ride:
That hour, o night's black arch the key-stane,
That dreary hour Tam mounts his beast in:
And sic a night he taks the road in,
As ne'er poor sinner was abroad in.

    The wind blew as 'twad blawn its last;
The rattling showers rose on the blast;
The speedy gleams the darkness swallow'd;
Loud, deep, and lang the thunder bellow'd;

That night, a child might understand,
The Deil had business on his hand.

    Weel mounted on his gray mare Meg,
A better never lifted leg,
Tam skelpit on thro dub and mire,
Despising wind, and rain, and fire;
Whiles holding fast his guid blue bonnet,
Whiles crooning o'er an auld Scots sonnet,
Whiles glow'ring round wi prudent cares,
Lest bogles catch him unawares:
Kirk-Alloway was drawing nigh,
Whare ghaists and houlets nightly cry.

    By this time he was cross the ford,
Whare in the snaw the chapman smoor'd;
And past the birks and meikle stane,
Whare drunken Charlie brak's neck-bane;
And thro the whins, and by the cairn,
Whare hunters fand the murder'd bairn;
And near the thorn, aboon the well,
Whare Mungo's mither hang'd hersel.
Before him Doon pours all his floods;
The doubling storm roars thro the woods;
The lightnings flash from pole to pole,
Near and more near the thunders roll:
When, glimmering thro the groaning trees,
Kirk-Alloway seem'd in a bleeze,
Thro ilka bore the beams were glancing,
And loud resounded mirth and dancing.

    Inspiring bold John Barleycorn,
What dangers thou canst make us scorn!
Wi tippenny, we fear nae evil;

skelpit – *spanked, hurried*
dub – *puddle*
boglies – *bogies*
ghaists and houlets
– *ghosts and owls*
smoor'd –
smothered
birks – *birches*
meikle – *big*
whins – *gorse*
ilka bore *every chink*
tippeny – *two-penny beer*

usquabae – *whisky*
noddle – *brain*
boddle – *farthing*
brent – *brand*

Wi usquabae, we'll face the Devil!
The swats sae ream'd in Tammie's noddle,
Fair play, he car'd na deils a boddle.
But Maggie stood, right sair astonish'd,
Till, by the heel and hand admonish'd,
She ventur'd forward on the light;
And, vow! Tam saw an unco sight!

    Warlocks and witches in a dance:
Nae cotillion, brent new frae France,
But hornpipes, jigs, strathspeys, and reels,

Tam o' Shanter – *an oil-painting by James Drummond*

Put life and mettle in their heels.
A winnock-bunker in the east,
There sat Auld Nick, in shape o beast;
A touzie tyke, black, grim and large,
To gie them music was his charge:
He screw'd the pipes and gart them skirl,
Till roof and rafters a' did dirl.
Coffins stood round, like open presses,
That shaw'd the dead in their last dresses;
And, by some devilish cantraip sleight,
Each in its cauld hand held a light:
By which heroic Tam was able
To note upon the haly table,
A murderer's banes, in gibbet-airns;
Twa span-lang, wee, unchristen'd bairns;
A thief new-cutted frae a rape –
Wi his last gasp his gab did gape;
Five tomahawks, wi bluid red-rusted,
Five scymitars, wi murder crusted;
A garter which a babe had strangled;
A knife a father's throat had mangled –
Whom his ain son o life bereft –
The grey-hairs yet stack to the heft;
Wi mair of horrible and awefu,
Which even to name wad be unlawfu.

    As Tammie glowr'd, amaz'd and curious,
The mirth and fun grew fast and furious,
The piper loud and louder blew,
The dancers quick and quicker flew,
They reel'd, they set, they cross'd, they cleekit,
Till ilka carlin swat and reekit,
And coost her duddies to the wark,
And linket at it in her sark!

winnock-bunker – *window-seat*
touzie tyke – *shaggy dog*
gart – *made*
skirl – *squeal*
dirl – *ring*
presses – *cupboards*
cantraip – *magic device*
-airns – *-irons*
bairns – *children*
rape – *rope*
gab – *mouth*
cleekit – *took hold*
ilka carlin swat and reekit – *every old witch sweated and steamed*
coost her duddies – *stripped off her clothes*
wark – *work*
linket – *tripped*
sark – *shift, chemise*

queans – *girls*
creeshie flannen –
greasy flannel
seventeen hunder
– *fine (1,700-
thread gauge)*
breeks – *breeches*
ance – *once*
hurdies – *buttocks*
ae blink – *a
glimpse*
burdies – *maidens*
rigwoodie –
withered
spean – *abort*
crummock –
cudgel
kend – *knew*
brawlie – *well*
wawlie – *choice*
core – *crew*
cutty sark – *short
shift*
Paisley harn –
coarse cloth
vauntie – *proud*
coft – *bought*
maun cour – *must
curb*

Now Tam, O Tam! had thae been queans,
A' plump and strapping in their teens!
Their sarks, instead o creeshie flannen,
Been snaw-white seventeen hunder linen! –
Thir breeks o mine, my only pair,
That ance were plush, o guid blue hair,
I wad hae gien them off my hurdies,
For ae blink o the bonie burdies!
But wither'd beldams, auld and droll,
Rigwoodie hags wad spean a foal,
Louping and flinging on a crummock,
I wonder did na turn thy stomach!

But Tam kend what was what fu brawlie:
There was ae winsome wench and wawlie,
That night enlisted in the core,
Lang after kend on Carrick shore
(For monie a beast to dead she shot,
And perish'd monie a bonie boat,
And shook baith meikle corn and bear,
And kept the country-side in fear).
Her cutty sark, o Paisley harn,
That while a lassie she had worn,
In longitude tho sorely scanty,
It was her best, and she was vauntie …
Ah! little kend thy reverend grannie,
That sark she coft for her wee Nannie,
Wi twa pund Scots ('twas a' her riches),
Wad ever grac'd a dance of witches!

But here my Muse her wing maun cour,
Sic flights are far beyond her power:
To sing how Nannie lap and flang

(A souple jade she was and strang),
And how Tam stood like ane bewitch'd,
And thought his very een enrich'd;
Even Satan glowr'd, and fidg'd fu fain,
And hotch'd and blew wi might and main:
Till first ae caper, syne anither,
Tam tint his reason a' thegither,
And roars out, 'Weel done, cutty sark!'
And in an instant all was dark:
And scarcely had he Maggie rallied,
When out the hellish legion sallied.

　　As bees bizz out wi angry fyke,
When plundering herds assail their byke;
As open pussie's mortal foes,
When, pop! she starts before their nose;
As eager runs the market-crowd,
When 'Catch the thief!' resounds aloud.
So Maggie runs, the witches follow,
Wi monie an eldritch skriech and hollow.

fain – *fondly*
hotch'd – *jerked*
syne – *then*
tint – *lost*
fyke – *fret*
byke – *hive*
pussie – *hare*
eldritch –
　unearthly

Figurehead of the Cutty
Sark *holding Meg's grey
tail. The tea clipper
was launched in
Dumbarton on the
River Clyde in 1869*

fairin – *deserts*
brig – *bridge*
fient – *never*
wist – *knew*
ettle – *aim,*
purpose
hale – *whole*
claught – *clawed*

Ah, Tam! Ah, Tam! thou'lt get thy fairin!
In hell they'll roast thee like a herrin!
In vain thy Kate awaits they comin!
Kate soon will be a woefu woman!
Now, do thy speedy utmost, Meg,
And win the key-stane of the brig;
There, at them thou thy tail may toss,
A running stream they dare na cross!
But ere the key-stane she could make,
The fient a tail she had to shake;
For Nannie, far before the rest,
Hard upon noble Maggie prest,
And flew at Tam wi furious ettle;
But little wist she Maggie's mettle –
Ae spring brought off her master hale,
But left behind her ain grey tail:
The carlin claught her by the rump,
And left poor Maggie scarce a stump.

Now, wha this tale o truth shall read,
Ilk man, and mother's son, take heed:
Whane'er to drink you are inclin'd,
Or cutty sarks run in your mind,
Think! ye may buy the joys o'er dear:
Remember Tam o Shanter's mare.

Moffat Water, Dumfries
and Galloway

My Wife's a Winsome Wee Thing

I never saw a fairer,
I never lo'ed a dearer,
And neist my heart I'll wear her,
    For fear my jewel tine.

Chorus
*She is a winsome wee thing,
She is a handsome wee thing,
She is a lo'esome wee thing,
    This sweet wee wife o mine!*

The warld's wrack we share o't;
The warstle and the care o't,
Wi her I'll blythely bear it,
    And think my lot divine.

wee – *little*

tine – *be lost*

neist – *next*

wrack – *wreckage*

warstle – *struggle*

*Above: Looking
towards Mouswald,
Dumfries and
Galloway*

Highland Mary

Ye banks and braes and streams around
    The castle o Montgomery,
Green be your woods, and fair your flowers,
    Your waters never drumlie!
There Summer first unfald her robes,
    And there the longest tarry!
For there I took the last fareweel
    O my sweet Highland Mary!

How sweetly bloom'd the gay, green birk,
    How rich the hawthorn's blossom,
As underneath their fragrant shade
    I clasp'd her to my bosom!
The golden hours on angel wings
    Flew o'er me and my dearie:
For dear to me as light and life
    Was my sweet Highland Mary.

Wi monie a vow and lock'd embrace
    Our parting was fu tender;
And, pledging aft to meet again,
    We tore oursels asunder.
But O! fell Death's untimely frost,
    That nipt my flower sae early!
Now green's the sod, and cauld's the clay,
    That wraps my Highland Mary!

O, pale, pale now, those rosy lips
    I aft hae kiss'd sae fondly;
And clos'd for ay, the sparkling glance
    That dwelt on me sae kindly;
And mouldering now in silent dust
    That heart that lo'ed me dearly!
But still within my bosom's core
    Shall live my Highland Mary.

*Opposite: W H Midwood's
painting of Burns
presenting a bible to
Mary Campbell*

To Mary in Heaven

Thou ling'ring star, with less'ning ray,
    That lov'st to greet the early morn,
Again thou usher'st in the day
    My Mary from my soul was torn.
O Mary dear departed shade!
    Where is thy place of blissful rest?
See'st thou thy lover lowly laid?
    Hear'st thou the groans that rend his breast?

That sacred hour can I forget?
    Can I forget the hallow'd grove,
Where, by the winding Ayr, we met,
    To live one day of parting love?
Eternity cannot efface
    Those records dear of transports past,
Thy image at our last embrace –
    Ah! little thought we 'twas our last!

Ayr, gurgling, kiss'd his pebbled shore,
    O'erhung with wild-woods, thickening green;
The fragrant birch and hawthorn hoar,
    'Twined amorous round the raptur'd scene;
The flowers sprang wanton to be prest,
    The birds sang love on every spray,
Till too, too soon, the glowing west,
    Proclaim'd the speed of winged day.

Still o'er these scenes my mem'ry wakes,
    And fondly broods with miser-care;
Time but th' impression stronger makes,
    As steams their channels deeper wear.
My Mary! dear departed shade!
    Where is they place of blissful rest?
See'st thou thy lover lowly laid?
    Hear'st thou the groans that rend his breast?

The Banks o Doon

Ye banks and braes o bonie Doon,
    How can ye bloom sae fresh and fair?
How can ye chant, ye little birds,
    And I sae weary, fu o care!
Thou'll break my heart, thou warbling bird,
    That wantons thro the flowering thorn!
Thou minds me o departed joys,
    Departed never to return.

Oft hae I rov'd by bonie Doon
    To see the rose and woodbine twine,
And ilka bird sang o its luve,
    And fondly sae did I o mine.
Wi lightsome heart I pu'd a rose,
    Fu sweet upon its thorny tree!
And my fause luver stole my rose –
    But ah! he left the thorn wi me.

Second version. This song illustrates a genuine experience: the heroine, a lovely and accomplished lady, was deserted by her lover after she had borne a son to him

braes – *slopes*
ilka – *every*

The Auld Brig o' Doon in Alloway

The Deil's awa wi th' Exciseman

ilka – *every*
maut – *malt*
braw – *fine*
meikle – *very*
(fine, great)

The Deil cam fiddlin thro the town,
  And danc'd awa wi th' Exciseman,
And ilka wife cries: 'Auld Mahoun,
  I wish you luck o' the prize, man!'

Chorus
The Deil's awa, the Deil's awa,
  The Deil's awa wi th' Exciseman!
He's danc'd awa, he's danc'd awa,
  He's danc'd awa wi th' Exciseman!

We'll mak our maut, we'll brew our drink,
  We'll laugh, sing, and rejoice, man,
And monie braw thanks to the meikle black Deil
  That danc'd awa wi th' Exciseman.

There's threesome reels, there's foursome reels,
  There's hornpipes and strathspeys, man,
But the ae best dance e'er cam to the land,
  Was the Deil's awa wi th' Exciseman.

*Chalk portrait of Robert
Burns by Archibald
Skirving (1749–1819)*

My Love, She's but a Lassie Yet

My love, she's but a lassie yet,
My love, she's but a lassie yet!
We'll let her stand a year or twa,
    She'll no be half sae saucy yet!
I rue the day I sought her, O!
I rue the day I sought her, O!
Wha gets her need na say he's woo'd,
    But he may say he has bought her, O.

    Come draw a drap o the best o't yet,
    Come draw a drap o the best o't yet!
Gae seek for pleasure whare ye will,
    But here I never miss'd it yet,
    We're a' dry wi drinkin o't,
    We're a' dry wi drinkin o't!
The minister kiss'd the fiddler's wife –
    He couldna preach for thinkin o't!

drap – *drop*
gae – *go*

*Above: Glentrool Forest
from Murray's
Monument, Dumfries
and Galloway*

Charlie, He's My Darling

The original was a street-ballad of about 1775, which Burns refined

jimped – *jumped*
tirl'd – *rattled on the latch*
brawlie weel – *finely*
kend – *knew*
scroggy – *scrubby*
daurna gang – *daren't go*

'Twas on a Monday morning
    Right early in the year,
That Charlie came to our town –
    The Young Chevalier!

Chorus
An Charlie he's my darling,
    My darling, my darling,
Charlie he's my darling –
    The Young Chevalier!

As he was walking up the street
    The city for to view,
O, there he spied a bonie lass
    The window looking thro!

Sae light's he jimped up the stair,
    And tirl'd at the pin;
And wha sae ready as hersel
    O let the laddie in!

He set his Jenny on his knee,
    All in his Highland dress;
For brawlie weel he kend the way
    To please a bonie lass.

It's up yon heathery mountain
    And down yon scroggy glen,
We daurna gang a-milking
    For Charlie and his men!

For the Sake o Somebody

My heart is sair – I dare na tell –
 My heart is sair for Somebody:
I could wake a winter night
 For the sake o Somebody.
  O-hon! for Somebody!
  O-hey! for Somebody!
I could range the world around
 For the sake o Somebody!'

Ye Powers that smile on virtuous love,
 O, sweetly smile on Somebody!
Frae ilka danger keep him free,
 And send me safe my Somebody!
  O-hon! for Somebody!
  O-hey! for Somebody!
I wad do – what wad I not? –
 For the sake o Somebody!

*'Somebody' was a synonym for **Bonnie Prince Charlie***

sair – *sore*
ilka – *every*

Portrait of Prince Charles Edward Stuart (Bonnie Prince Charlie, 1720–88) from the Leith Hall collection

To a Louse

*On seeing one on
a lady's bonnet
at church*

crowlin ferlie –
crawling marvel

strunt – *strut*

fit – *foot*

swith! – *off!*

haffet – *side-locks
of hair*

squattle – *squat*

sprattle – *scramble*

horn nor bane –
*horn nor bone
comb*

*The River Tay from
Kinnoull Hill, near
Perth*

Ha! whare ye gaun', ye crowlin ferlie?
Your impudence protects you sairly;
I canna say but ye strunt rarely
    Owre gauze and lace,
Tho faith! I fear ye dine but sparely
    On sic a place.

Ye ugly, creepin, blastit wonner,
Detested, shunn'd by saunt and sinner,
How daur ye set a fit upon her –
    Sae fine a lady!
Gae somewhere else and seek your dinner
    On some poor body.

Swith! in some beggar's haffet squattle;
There ye may creep, and sprawl, and sprattle,
Wi ither kindred, jumping cattle;
    In shoals and nations;
Whare horn nor bane ne'er daur unsettle
    Your thick plantations.

Now haud you there! ye're out o sight,
Below the fatt'rels, snug an tight,
Na, faith ye yet! ye'll no be right,
    Till ye've got on it –
The vera tapmost, tow'rin height
    O Miss's bonnet.

My sooth! right bauld yet set your nose out,
As plump an gray as onie grozet:
O for some rank, mercurial rozet,
    Or fell, red smeddum,
I'd gie you sic a hearty dose o't,
    Wad dress your droddum!

I wadna been surpris'd to spy
You on an auld wife's flainen toy;
Or aiblins some bit duddie boy,
    On's wyliecoat;
But Miss's fine Lunardi! fye!
    How daur ye do't?

O Jenny, dinna toss your head,
An set your beauties a' abread!
Ye little ken what cursed speed
    The blastie's makin!
Thae winks an finger-ends, I dread,
    Are notice takin!

O wad some Power the giftie gie us
To see oursels as ithers see us!
It wad frae monie a blunder free us,
    An foolish notion:
What airs in dress an gait wad lea'e us,
    An ev'n devotion!

fatt'rels – *falderols*

grozet – *goose-berry*

rozet – *resin*

smeddum – *deadly powder*

droddum – *back-side*

flainen toy – *flannel cap*

aiblins – *perhaps*

duddie – *ragged*

wyliecoat – *ragged vest*

Lunardi – *fashionable balloon bonnet*

abread – *abroad*

blastie – *pest*

thae – *those*

Rantin, Rovin Robin

When the poet's father was riding to fetch a doctor to assist at Robert's birth, he helped an old gypsy woman to cross a flooded stream. In gratitude she visited the new-born child and made the predictions incorporated in this song

rantin – *merry*

hansel – *birth gift*

gossip – *old woman*

keekit – *peered*

loof – *face*

waly – *sturdy*

coof – *fool*

ilka – *every*

leeze – *blessings*

gar – *make*

aspar – *legs apart*

fauts – *faults*

waur – *worse*

Opposite: The Pass of Killiecrankie, Perth and Kinross

There was a lad was born in Kyle,
But whatna day o whatna style,
I doubt it's hardly worth the while
    To be sae nice wi Robin.

Chorus
Robin was a rovin boy,
    Rantin rovin, rantin rovin,
Robin was a rovin boy,
    Rantin, rovin Robin!

Our monarch's hindmost year but ane
Was five-and-twenty days begun,
'Twas then a blast o Janwar win'
    Blew hansel in on Robin.

The gossip keekit in his loof,
Quo she: 'Wha lives will see the proof,
This waly boy will be nae coof:
    I think we'll ca' him Robin.'

'He'll hae misfortunes great an sma
But ay a heart aboon them a'.
He'll be a credit till us a':
    We'll a' be proud o Robin!'

'But sure as three times three mak nine,
I see by ilka score and line,
This chap will dearly like our kin',
    So leeze me on thee, Robin.'

'Guid faith', quo she, 'I doubt you, sir,
Ye'll gar the lasses lie aspar;
But twenty fauts ye may hae waur –
    So blessins on thee, Robin!'

To a Mountain Daisy

*On turning
one down with
a plough in
April 1786*

stoure – *dust*

wa's – *walls*

bield – *shelter*

histie – *bare*

Wee, modest, crimson-tippèd flow'r,
Thou's met me in an evil hour;
For I maun crush amang the stoure
    Thy slender stem:
To spare thee now is past my pow'r,
    Thou bonie gem.

Alas! it's no thy neebor sweet,
The bonie lark companion meet,
Bending thee 'mang the dewy weet,
    Wi spreckl'd beast!
When upward-springing, blythe, to greet
    The purpling east.

Cauld blew the bitter-biting north
Upon they early, humble birth;
Yet cheerfully thou glinted forth
    Amid the storm,
Scarce rear'd above the parent-earth
    Thy tender form.

The flaunting flow'rs our gardens yield,
High shelt'ring woods and wa's maun shield;
But thou, beneath the random bield
    O clod or stane,
Adorns the histie stibble-field,
    Unseen, alane.

There, in thy scanty mantle clad,
Thy snawie bosom sun-ward spread,
Thou lifts thy unassuming head
    In humble guise;
But now the share uptears thy bed,
    And low thou lies!

Such is the fate of artless maid,
Sweet flow'ret of the rural shade!
By love's simplicity betray'd,
     And guileless trust;
Till she, like thee, all soil'd, is laid
     Low i' the dust.

Such is the fate of simple Bard,
On Life's rough ocean luckless starr'd!
Unskilful he to note the card
     Of prudent lore,
Till billows rage, and gales blow hard,
     And whelm him o'er!

Such fate to suffering Worth is giv'n,
Who long with wants and woes has
     striv'n,
By human pride or cunning driv'n
     To mis'ry's brink;
Till, wrench'd of ev'ry stay but Heav'n,
     He, ruin'd, sink!

Ev'n thou who mourn'st the Daisy's fate,
That fate is thine – no distant date;
Stern Ruin's plough-share drives elate,
     Full on thy bloom,
Till crush'd beneath the furrow's weight,
     Shall be thy doom!

Killiecrankie

This song com-
memorates the
battle where
Viscount Dundee
fell in the moment
of victory. The
chorus is old

braw – *fine*

brankie – *spruce*

cantie – *merry*

braes – *hills*

furr – *ditch*

clankie – *knock*

gled – *hawk*

Chorus
An ye had been whare I hae been,
  Ye wad na been sae cantie, O!
An ye had seen what I hae seen,
  I' the braes o Killiecrankie, O!

'Whare hae ye been sae braw, lad?
  Whare hae ye been sae brankie, O?
Whare hae ye been sae braw, lad?
  Cam ye by Killiecrankie, O?

'I faught at land, I faught at sea,
  At hame I faught my auntie, O;
But I met the Devil an Dundee,
  On the braes o' Killiecrankie, O.

'The bauld Pitcur fell in a furr,
An Clavers gat a clankie, O,
Or I had fed an Athole gled,
On the braes o Killiecrankie, O!'

*Above: The Pass of
Killiecrankie,
Perth and Kinross*

84

Bonie Dundee

Selected verses

'My blessin's upon thy sweet, wee lippie!
  My blessin's upon thy bonie e'e-brie!
Thy smiles are sae like my blythe sodger laddie,
  Thou's ay be the dearer and dearer to me!

'But I'll big a bow'r on yon bonie banks,
  Whare Tay rins wimplin by sae clear;
An I'll cleed thee in the tartan sae fine,
  An mak thee a man like thy daddie dear.'

e'e-brie – *eyebrow*
sodger – *soldier*
big – *build*
wimplin – *mean-dering*
cleed – *clothe*

Below: The body of John Graham of Claverhouse, Viscount Dundee, being carried from the battlefield at Killiecrankie (1689)

Comin thro the Rye

draigl't – *soiled*

gin – *if*

ken – *know*

*Ayrshire farmland
near Mauchline*

Comin thro the rye, poor body,
    Comin thro the rye,
She draigl't a' her petticoatie,
    Comin thro the rye!

Chorus
O, Jenny's a' sweet, poor body,
    Jenny's seldom dry:
She draigl't a' her petticoatie,
    Comin thro the rye!

Gin a body meet a body
    Comin thro the rye,
Gin a body kiss a body,
    Need a body cry?

Gin a body meet a body
    Coming thro the glen,
Gin a body kiss a body,
    Need the warld ken?

***Burns wrote this varied
rendering of one of the verses
with a diamond on a window-
pane, which can still be seen at
the Globe Inn, Dumfries***

Gin a body meet a body
    Coming thro the grain
Gin a body kiss a body
    The thing's a body's ain.

Address to a Haggis

Fair fa' your honest, sonsie face,
Great chieftain o the puddin-race!
Aboon them a' ye tak your place,
    Painch, tripe, or thairm:
Weel are ye wordy of a grace
    As lang's my arm.

The groaning trencher there ye fill,
Your hurdies like a distant hill,
Your pin wad help to mend a mill
    In time o need,
While thro your pores the dews distil
    Like amber bead.

His knife see rustic Labour dight,
An cut you up wi ready slight,
Trenching your gushing entrails bright,
    Like onie ditch;
And then, O what a glorious sight,
    Warm-reekin, rich!

Then, horn for horn, they stretch an strive:
Deil tak the hindmost, on they drive,
Till a' their weel-swall'd kytes belyve
    Are bent like drums;
Then auld Guidman, maist like to rive,
    'Bethankit' hums.

Is there that owre his French *ragout,*
Or *olio* that wad staw a sow,
Or *fricassee* wad mak he spew
    Wi perfect sconner,
Looks down wi sneering, scornfu view
    On sic a dinner?

The haggis, a very palatable Scottish dish, is made from minced offal of mutton, meal, suet and seasoning, and boiled in a sheep's stomach

fair fa' – *good luck to*
sonsie – *cheerful*
painch – *paunch*
thairm – *guts*
pin – *skewer*
hurdies – *hips*
dight – *wipe*
slight – *skill*
reekin – *steaming*
horn – *horn spoon*
weel-swall'd kytes – *well-swollen bellies*
belyve – *soon*
rive – *burst*
staw – *sicken*
sconner – *disgust*

87

feckless – *weak*

rash – *thin stalk of a marsh plant*

nieve – *fist*

nit – *head-louse egg*

walie – *huge, large*

sned – *chop off*

taps o thrissle – *thistle tops*

skinking – *watery*

jaups – *splashes*

luggies – *milking-pails*

Poor devil! see him owre his trash,
As feckless as a wither'd rash,
His spindle shank a guid whip-lash,
 His nieve a nit;
Thro bloody flood or field to dash,
 O how unfit!

But mark the Rustic, haggis-fed,
The trembling earth resounds his tread,
Clap in his walie nieve a blade,
 He'll mak it whissle;
An legs an arms, an heads will sned,
 Like taps o thrissle.

Ye Pow'rs, wha mak mankind your care,
An dish them out their bill o fare,
Auld Scotland wants nae skinking ware
 That jaups in luggies;
But, if ye wish her gratefu prayer,
 Gie her a Haggis!

The Haggis Feast, *oil-painting by Alexander Fraser,* ARSA *(1786–1865)*

Highland Laddie

She:
The bonniest lad that e'er I saw,
    Bonie laddie, Highland laddie,
Wore a plaid and was fu braw,
    Bonie Highland laddie.

On his head a bonnet blue,
    Bonie laddie, Highland laddie;
His royal heart was firm and true,
    Bonie Highland laddie.

He:
Trumpets sound and cannons roar,
    Bonie lassie, Lawland lassie,
And a' the hills wi echoes roar,
    Bonie Lawland lassie.

Glory, honour, now invite
    Bonie lassie, Lawland lassie,
For freedom and my King to fight,
    Bonie Lawland lassie.

She:
The sun a backward course shall take,
    Bonie laddie, Highland laddie,
Ere aught thy manly courage shake;
    Bonie Highland laddie.

Go, for yourself procure renown,
    Bonie laddie, Highland laddic,
And for your lawful King his crown,
    Bonie Highland laddie.

An improvement and expansion of 'The Highland Lad and the Lowland Lassie'

braw – *fine, handsome*
Lawland – *Lowland*

The Rantin Dog, the Daddie o't

Written for Elizabeth Paton, a servant in Burns' mother's house

rantin – *rollicking*

babie-clouts – *baby-linen*

tent – *attend to*

faut – *fault*

maut – *ale to drink to child's birth*

ca't – *name it*

creepie-chair – *stool of repentance*

crack – *talk*

my lane – *alone*

fidgin fain – *fidget with delight*

O, wha my babie-clouts will buy?
O, wha will tent me when I cry?
Wha will kiss me where I lie? –
 The rantin dog, the daddie o't!

O, wha will own he did the faut?
O, wha will buy the groanin maut?
O, wha will tell me how to ca't? –
 The rantin dog, the daddie o't!

When I mount the creepie-chair,
Wha will sit beside me there?
Gie me Rob, I'll seek nae mair –
 The rantin dog, the daddie o't!

Wha will crack to me my lane?
Wha will mak me fidgin fain?
Wha will kiss me o'er again? –
 The rantin dog, the daddie o't!

Above: River Tummel, near Pitlochry

90

The Selkirk Grace

Some have meat and cannot eat.
 Some cannot eat that want it:
But we have meat and we can eat,
 Sae let the Lord be thankit.

An impromptu verse on being asked to say grace at dinner while visiting the Earl of Selkirk

Border scenery near Selkirk

Address to the Toothache

Written when the author was grievously tormented by that disorder

stang – *sting*

lug – *ear*

twang – *twinge*

slavers – *saliva*

giglets – *children*

keckle – *cackle*

loup – *dance*

heckle – *flax comb*

doup – *backside*

dools – *sorrows*

hairsts – *harvests*

cutty-stools – *stools of repentance*

mools – *crumbling earth*

fash – *annoyance*

gree – *prize*

raw – *row*

My curse upon your venom'd stang,
That shoots my tortur'd gums alang,
An thro my luggies monie a twang
    Wi gnawing vengeance,
Tearing my nerves wi bitter pang,
    Like racking engines!

A'down my beard the slavers trickle,
I throw the wee stools o'er the meikle,
While round the fire the giglets keckle,
    To see me loup,
An raving mad, I wish a heckle
    Were i' their doup!

When fevers burn, or ague freezes,
Rheumatics gnaw, or cholic squeezes,
Our neebors sympathise to ease us,
    Wi pitying moan;
But thee! – thou hell o a' diseases –
    They mock our groan!

Of a' the numerous human dools –
Ill-hairsts, daft bargains, cutty-stools,
Or worthy frien's laid i' the mools,
    Sad sight to see!
The tricks o knaves, or fash o fools –
    Thou bear'st the gree!

Whare'er that place be priests ca' Hell,
Whare a' the tones o misery yell,
An ranked plagues their numbers tell,
    In dreadfu raw,
Thou, Toothache, surely bear'st the bell,
    Amang them a'!

O thou grim, mischief-making chiel,
That gars the notes o discord squeel,
Till human kind aft dance a reel
    In gore, a shoe-thick,
Gie a' the faes o Scotland's weal
    A towmond's toothache!

gars – *makes*
gie – *give*
faes – *foes*
weal – *welfare*
towmond – *twelve months*

The River Tay near Dunkeld, Perth and Kinross

My Luve is Like a Red, Red Rose

*This is an
amalgam of
several old ballads*

O, my luve is like a red, red rose,
    That's newly sprung in June.
O, my luve's like the melodie,
    That's sweetly play'd in tune.

As fair art thou, my bonie lass,
    So deep in luve am I,
And I will luve thee still, my dear,
    Till a' the seas gang dry.

Till a' the seas gang dry, my dear,
    And the rocks melt wi the sun!
And I will luve thee still, my dear,
    While the sands o life shall run.

And fare thee weel, my only luve!
    And fare thee weel, a while!
And I will come again, my luve,
    Tho it were ten thousand mile!

Rosa 'Danse du Feu'

Lines

Admiring Nature in her wildest grace,
These northern scenes with weary feet I trace;
O'er many a winding dale and painful steep,
Th' abodes of covey'd grouse and timid sheep,
My savage journey, curious, I pursue,
Till fam'd Breadalbane opens to my view.
The meeting cliffs each deep-sunk glen divides:
The woods, wild-scatter'd, clothe their ample sides;
Th' outstretching lake, imbosomed 'mong the hills,
The eye with wonder and amazement fills:
The Tay meandering sweet in infant pride,
The palace rising on its verdant side,
The lawns, wood-fring'd in Nature's native taste,
The hillocks dropt in Nature's careless haste,
The arches striding o'er the new-born stream,
The village glittering in the noontide beam –

Poetic ardors in my bosom swell,
Lone wand'ring by the hermit's mossy cell;
The sweeping theatre of hanging woods,
Th' incessant roar of headlong tumbling floods –

Here Poesy might wake her heav'n-taught lyre,
And look through Nature with creative fire;
Here, to the wrongs of Fate half-reconcil'd,
Misfortune's lighten'd steps might wander wild;
And Disappointment, in these lonely bounds,
Find balm to soothe her bitter rankling wounds;
Here heart-struck Grief might heav'nward stretch
    her scan,
And injur'd Worth forget and pardon man.

Also known as 'Verses Written with a Pencil' – over the chimney-piece in the parlour of the inn at Kenmore, Taymouth

Auld Lang Syne

Burns first sent this famous song to his friend Mrs Dunlop on 7 December 1788; he wrote: 'Is not the phrase "Auld Lang Syne" exceedingly impressive', and when he eventually sent it to George Thomson of Dumfries, he finished his letter with, 'one more song and I am done, "Auld Lang Syne".'

auld lang syne –
old long ago
stowp – *tankard*
braes – *hillsides*
pou'd – *pulled*
gowans – *daisies*
braid – *broad*
fiere – *friend*
guid-willie waught
– *goodwill draught*

Should auld acquaintance be forgot,
 And never brought to mind?
Should auld acquaintance be forgot,
 And auld lang syne?

Chorus
For auld lang syne, my dear,
For auld lang syne,
We'll tak a cup o kindness yet,
For auld lang syne!

And surely ye'll be your pint-stowp,
 And surely I'll be mine,
And we'll tak a cup o kindness yet,
 For auld lang syne!

We twa hae run about the braes,
 And pou'd the gowans fine,
But we've wander'd monie a weary fit,
 Sin auld lang syne.

We twa hae paidl'd in the burn
 Frae morning sun till dine,
But seas between us braid hae roar'd
 Sin auld lang syne.

And there's a hand my trusty fiere,
 And gie's a hand o thine,
And we'll tak a right guid-willie waught,
 For auld lang syne.